In The Garden

An Ordinary Women, An Extraordinary Life

Ellen – A Memoir

Second Edition

by Janet (VanGunst) Hasselbring

PRINCIPIA
MEDIA

In The Garden
© 2013 Jan Hasselbring
Published by Principia Media, LLC, Wyoming, MI
www.principiamedia.com

ISBN 978-1-61485-314-5

All rights reserved. No part of this book may be reproduced or transmitted in any form by any means, electronic or mechanical, including photocopying and recording, or by any information storage and retrieval system, except as may be expressly permitted by the 1976 Copyright Act or by the publisher. Requests for permission should be made in writing to:
Principia Media, LLC
678 Front Ave. N.W,
Suite 256
Grand Rapids MI 49504

Disclaimer: Certain names, identifying details and events have been changed to protect the privacy of individuals. The author has faithfully tried to recreate events, locales and conversations often from memory. Although the author and publisher have made every effort to ensure that the information in this book is correct, the author and publisher do not assume and hereby disclaim any liability to any party for any loss, damage, or disruption caused by errors or omissions, whether such errors or omissions result from negligence, accident, or other cause.

Scripture quotations, unless otherwise noted, are taken from the Holy Bible, King James Version, Cambridge, 1769.

Scripture quotations marked "NIV" are taken from HOLY BIBLE, NEW INTERNATIONAL VERSION. Copyright 1973, 1978, 1984 by International Bible Society. Used by permission of Zondervan Publishing House.

Cover illustration courtesy of Bruce DeVries
Cover and interior design by Jerry Lee

Printed in the United States of America

19 18 17 16 15 14 13   7 6 5 4 3 2 1

"Next to the might of God,

the serene beauty of a holy life is the

most powerful influence for good in the world."

Dwight L. Moody

dedicated to
my brothers and sisters
our children
grandchildren
great grandchildren
and all those yet to come

may Ellen's story never
be forgotten

TABLE OF CONTENTS

vii	Preface
13	God Will Provide
65	Accepting The Unacceptable
74	The Pain Of Estrangement
85	Heaven Tugging, Always Tugging
92	Home At Last
109	Final Gifts
135	Memories Of Loved Ones
172	A Final Word
189	Appendix - An Invitation
194	Appendix - A Challenge
197	Photo Album
213	Family Tree – Ellen and Henry VanGunst
218	Study Guide I
224	Study Guide II

PREFACE

Lighting The Match

"You always stare at the window of the one you love." [1]

    My mother died on September 1, 2005. I'm not sure when the idea of writing her story came to me, but I suspect it's been germinating for some time.

    Perhaps the seed was sown as I watched her die. I sat transfixed by her bedside, as I heard her, on more than one occasion, talking lucidly with my father, Henry, who had preceded her in death. It seemed she was traveling back and forth along the pathway to heaven before her final departure from this life. I realized, with some amazement, that my father was waiting, along with the angels, to guide her home at the moment of her death. Watching her die changed my life.

    My mother was not afraid of death - in fact, toward the end, she embraced and welcomed death, because she was certain she was going to heaven to be reunited with her loved ones and her Lord. She died peacefully and victoriously. As I reflected on this, I suspected there was a close correlation between the way she had lived her life and the peace and certainty she exhibited at the end.

    Aging sobers us. If I live to be ninety, like my mother, I have entered the third and last trimester of my life. I have experienced many of the same vicissitudes of life she did – childhood, adolescence, marriage, having children, making a living, menopause, loss of dear ones, depression, suffering, aging and the imminence of my own death.

Because I have children I can appreciate the challenges my mother faced in tending a family and the pain and suffering she experienced when she lost a beloved daughter and became estranged from her youngest son. I cannot imagine how I would cope in similar situations. I do not know how I will deal with the death of my husband, living alone, failing health, old age and finally, death.

My mother knew all of this and yet she died a mellow, gentle child of God. Her faith, devotion, and love saw her through grief and loneliness. Her death was not the end - it was a beginning. The more I reflected on her life, the more I came to appreciate and respect her. I found myself wanting to learn more about her and to be like her - to be a model for my children and grandchildren, as she was, and continues to be, for me.

I wanted my children and grandchildren to know her story. I found it fascinating and didn't want it to be forgotten. Her story seemed like a candle in the darkness, lighting the way to hope and faith.

I thought, I reflected, and I pondered...

The pen was poised, but the match was still unlit...

Then, one morning, about five years after her death, I was having coffee with a friend. We were solving the problems of the day when our discussion turned to spiritual matters. I don't remember what triggered my comments, but I began talking about my mother. I mentioned that her faith had brought her through the defining moments of her life. I described her marvelous and peaceful journey into heaven.

"I wish I could have a faith like that," my friend said, wistfully.

"Oh, but you can," I said, somewhat taken aback.

"No, no - it's too late for me," she insisted.

I'm not one to proselytize, but her reply upset me.

"It's never too late to find faith - to find God."

Flailing about for something convincing, I relayed what I had learned from reading *The Great Divorce* by C.S. Lewis.

This powerful allegory demonstrates that God never turns anyone away, but we, by the choices we make at the forks in the roads of our lives, turn away from Him. In his book, Lewis describes a busload of souls on their way to heaven. When they arrive in the heavenly heights they have the opportunity to get off the bus and remain but only one brave soul chooses to stay. The rest climb back on the bus and return to their homes below. They cannot tolerate the rigors of the light, preferring instead the comfortable meaningless of life in the gray "Shadowlands," as Lewis describes their earthly abode. Lewis also states that if we live too long in the gray areas and shut God out of our lives, our hearts can become hardened to the light of God's grace and mercy. This was true for the passengers who returned, but I didn't want to think it was true for my friend.

"So you see," I said triumphantly, thinking I had proven my point, "it's not too late."

"Yes, it is," she said firmly, undeterred. "I'm past that point in my life. Trust me. It's too late for me to change." Then after a pause, "Tell me more about your mother."

So I told her about my mother - how she dealt with suffering and pain, how she never forsook her Jesus and how her faith brought her peace at the end. I described again her marvelous entry to heaven, where I knew she was interceding and praying for her loved ones.

When I was finished my friend looked at me.

"You should write your mother's story," she said. "It is

powerful and you obviously feel very strongly about it. I'd like to read it when you're finished."

After she left I reflected on our conversation. Although she was adamant in her unbelief, I felt a flicker of hope. She had wanted to hear about my mother. She had asked to read her story. Could my mother's story possibly help her find the faith she believed was beyond her grasp?

I think it was at that moment I knew I must write this memoir – not just for myself and for my family, but for those who might find in it a ray of hope, a glimmer of faith.

A few months later I had another encounter, which helped to solidify my resolve. A friend's son had died tragically and unexpectedly. My friend and her husband were grief stricken. I called and sent a card to let them know I was praying for them. I know enough about grief to know that when people are suffering, the last thing they want to hear is, "I know how you feel." They just need for you to be there - to listen, to care, to share in their pain.

After some time had passed, I mentioned to my friend that my mother had also lost an adult child and described how her faith had helped her cope with her grief. I knew that it was too soon to be of much help but I mentioned that I was writing my mother's memoir and if she were interested I'd share it with her.

A couple months later I saw her again.

"I think I'm ready to read your memoir," she said as we parted that day. Once again, I marveled to think that my mother's story might help bring comfort to a fellow sufferer.

It's been said that "you can't write about something until ten years afterward...it takes that amount of time to gain aesthetic distance or you merely do cooked-up journalism. "[2]

Ignoring that advice, I pick up the pen, strike the match

and begin to write. May this memoir be a candle glowing in the darkness of unbelief and suffering.

♥

CHAPTER ONE

God Will Provide

"...built an house, and digged deep, and laid the foundation on a rock..." Luke 6:48

If there was a defining moment in my mother's life, it was when she met, courted and married Henry VanGunst.

"Therefore, shall a man leave his father and his mother and shall cleave to his wife: and they shall be one flesh." Gen. 2:24

Henry and Ellen were married March 12, 1936 in New Era, Michigan. Their wedding anniversary would be an historic one.

It was the day Hitler broke the Treaty of Versailles and sent troops into Rhineland, gearing up his Nazi regime. Later that summer his evil dictatorship scored a huge propaganda success as host of the Summer Olympics in Berlin, where American sprinter, Jessie Owens would set a 100-meter record at 10.2 seconds and would go on to win 4 Olympic gold medals. That month the Boulder Dam (later called the Hoover) was completed and the airship, the

Hindenburg, made its first flight in Germany. This was the year Chiang Kai-shek's troops conquered Kanton and declared war on Japan and civil war broke out in Spain. Margaret Mitchell's "Gone With the Wind" was published and the Triborough Bridge connecting Queens, the Bronx and Manhattan opened. The first transatlantic round-trip air flight occurred and in the fall of that year, the radio would be used for the first time in the presidential campaign, which FDR won in a landslide against Republican, Alfred M. Landon.

The first issue of LIFE magazine appeared. Its cover showed an obstetrician slapping a newborn baby and a caption with these words: "LIFE Begins on This Day in History."

And LIFE began for Henry and Ellen on the day they spoke their vows at the altar. Their relationship would last over 60 years and would become a cornerstone in the history of their family.

"I, Ellen, take you Henry, to be my lawfully, wedded husband. I promise to love you, honor you, and cherish you in this relationship and leaving all others, cleave only unto you, in all things a true and faithful wife so long as we both shall live, in the name of the Father, the Son and the Holy Spirit. Amen." (Traditional wedding vows)

After their honeymoon to the Wisconsin Dells, they returned to the farm and the house Henry had built for his bride. It sat on a hill, overlooking the countryside, next door to Henry's parents, Andrew and Jane VanGunst.

When Henry, ever the romantic, scooped up his petite bride (all 5'4" and 90 lbs. of her), carried her across the threshold, up the back stairway and deposited her gently on the kitchen floor, their life together officially began.

Their lives would be fashioned and shaped by that house

on the farm, but, in return, the farm would forever bear the stamp of their presence.

Henry grew up on the farm. He was the only son of four children. He worked for his father, Andrew, and always planned to take over the farm one day. Ellen was a city girl from New Era, Michigan. Their lives were similar in some ways; however, a look at their family histories reveals very different backgrounds.

Henry wanted Ellen to develop a love for the farm and often shared his family's history and recounted stories of growing up with her.

Henry's father, Andrew VanGunst, came to America with his family from Friesland, the Netherlands. Within a year, his family members - both parents and a sibling, died from tuberculosis, or consumption, as it was called then.

He recounted how Andrew, now an orphan, moved to Fremont, Michigan, to live with an uncle who had come to America with them. He worked on his uncle's farm in exchange for room and board. His uncle gave him two bull calves. For three years Andrew raised and trained his calves, intending to use them as oxen to help clear land when he purchased a farm of his own. One day he came home from a trip to town and went out to visit the calves. To his surprise, the stalls were empty. When he asked his uncle the whereabouts of the calves, he was told they had been sold to pay off farm debts.

Feeling betrayed and heartbroken, Andrew left his uncle and went to live with the VanderWall family just north of New Era, Michigan. He stayed there until 1901 when, at age 21, he bought 40-acres of virgin land about a mile further north.

There was a small house on the property, but no barn. A family, by the name of Westfield, owned a farm across the road. They had a barn but no house, so they lived with Andrew until their house was built. In return, Andrew used their barn.

Andrew had 6 milk cows and a team of horses to work the land. There were apple trees on the property when he purchased it, and over time, he planted cherry trees and raised corn, potatoes, and hay.

When he built a new house, he bought a second team of horses to haul the lumber from a sawmill 10 miles away. He hired a worker who did the field work while he transported the lumber. The two carpenters, who built the house, were each paid $3.00 a day. The stonemason, who laid the foundation, charged $3.00 for a 10-hour day.

Andrew married Jennie (Jane) Grinwis. They had four children - three daughters and a son - Henry, born in 1909.

By now the farm was 80 acres in size. As a child, Henry milked the cows by hand and worked in the fields with the horses. He picked cherries during the summer and potatoes in the fall. Farm children were given two weeks off from school to help with the potato harvest. He helped his mother, Jane, with her flock of chickens. The eggs she sold provided money for groceries.

Henry loved to tell Ellen about his father's spirited horse, Bell. When the family went to church on Sundays or the children went to catechism class on Saturday mornings, Andrew would drive them in the horse and buggy or in the cutter, during the winter. When it was time to leave, Andrew would circle round and round the yard with Bell as Jane tossed the children into the buggy one at a time. Finally, free to run, Bell hit the open road. She could cover the mile and a half to town in less than five minutes.

When the farm across the street changed hands, Henry gained a childhood friend. The new owners, the Wickstras, had a son, Pete, who was his age. Henry and Pete had many good times together. They tapped maple trees in the spring and hauled the sap in milk cans from the woods in a coaster wagon. They trained Henry's dog to pull the heavy wagon. If he balked, they got a cat from the barn and threw it ahead of the wagon to get him going. Henry's mother, Jane, boiled the sap until it became maple syrup, which the boys sold for spending money.

They brought the cows to pasture in the mornings and back again in the evenings for their second milking.

Sometimes after school, Henry and Pete would catch the freight train at the depot in New Era and ride it home, jumping off before the track began the steep downhill grade. Their school class visited local resident, Mr. J. C. Hamm and listened to a radio for the first time.

Henry had an uncle who worked for the local grocery store. He drove a peddle wagon - a covered wagon, pulled by a team of horses, containing groceries and other household items. He would start out on Monday morning and be gone all week, spending the evenings at various farmhouses on his route. He and his family would visit Andrew and Jane on Saturday afternoons. His boys needed watching because they would run loose on the farm. They let the chickens out of the chicken coop and pestered the pigs.

Henry told her about the time when Jane's relatives came for a visit. One of the men, who owned a Model T Ford, wanted to try out Andrew's 1917 Dodge. The problem was that the gas lever on the Dodge worked just the opposite of the one on his car so when he tried to stop, he became confused and went faster instead. He drove furiously around and around the yard, circling an apple tree. He finally slammed into the tree, bringing down an avalanche of apples and seriously damaging Andrew's car. The driver was white with fright but not injured. That was one of Ellen's favorite tales.

Coming to America from another country, losing his parents and a sibling and starting a farm at age 21 from 80 acres of grassland, a few apple trees, lots of weeds and a host of trees to cut down, took faith, courage, hard work and diligence on Andrew's part - traits Henry surely imbibed as he worked with his father from the time he was young.

Ellen's parents had come from the Netherlands too. Her mother, Winnie, was born in Friesland and her father, Benjamin, hailed from Gronigen, the Netherlands. Benjamin's parents died when he was young so Ellen did not know them; however, her mother's parents lived nearby on a farm and Ellen spent lots of time with them. The local school - Batten School, was named after them.

Benjamin and his brother John owned the local hardware store. John handled the sales and service of the machinery and farm tools while Benjamin took care of the books and office details. During the depression they accepted produce, such as apples, potatoes, dry beans, etc., in exchange for merchandise. One man paid off his bill by building a cottage for Benjamin on property he owned on nearby Stony Lake. The cottage was witness to the piecemeal fashion in which the bill was paid.

On Christmas Eve, 1931, John Postema and his family met a tragic end. John, his wife, Rika and their three children were in Chicago visiting Rika's sister's family. Rika's sister's husband was a sailor and was taking care of a friend's boat for the winter. The boat was docked near the loading area for large grain ships along the Chicago River. It was a treacherous evening with blinding snow, sleet and icy road conditions. After attending a late evening Christmas Eve service, they returned to the docks. John was attempting to turn the car around when he made too short a turn and the car slid into the deep icy waters. Everyone inside the car - the entire family, drowned. Only the sailor, Rika's sister's husband, who was standing on the running board helping John navigate the dangerous turn, survived. The bodies were returned to New Era for a family funeral and burial.

Benjamin and Winnie lived above the hardware store until Benjamin purchased a large, two story, five-bedroom house from a local grocer. It was one of the few houses in New Era to have indoor plumbing at that time. Ellen was visiting an aunt in Muskegon, Michigan and remembered being pleasantly surprised, upon her return, to find that her family had moved to a new house!

Ellen, like Henry, had many fond childhood memories. Once, she and her older sister, Marie, went to the creek to play. The creek ran just behind the hardware store. Both girls fell in, Ellen headfirst. They went home, hurt and bleeding (Ellen had the scar to prove it).

Ellen often did errands for her Grandpa and Grandma Battan. They lived across the railroad tracks. One day she was visiting them to get their grocery list, when she came upon the freight train stopped on the tracks. She crawled under and went on her way; however, her father, Benjamin had seen her from his office in the store and gave her a sound spanking - the only spanking she ever remembered getting from him.

There were signs early on that Ellen was bright, talented and full of initiative. She skipped 1st grade upon the recommendation of her teacher. She was the valedictorian in both the 8th and 10th grades. In high school she was enrolled in a business course. She excelled in typing class and entered the state typing contest and came in sixth in the state. She was offered a scholarship to Davenport Business Institute in Grand Rapids, Michigan, but her father didn't want her to go to the big city so she stayed home and worked for him in the hardware store instead.

Ellen loved playing a piano that was for sale in the hardware store. Seeing her talent and love for music, Benjamin had the piano brought to their home. Ellen took piano lessons and when she was in the 8th grade, her piano teacher entered her in a statewide competition. She won first place over several 10th grade girls and was awarded a manicure set in a leather case - an award she treasured.

She learned to play the organ also. Her Grandpa and Grandma Batten had a pump organ in their house, which Ellen played whenever she went to visit. In the winter the parlor was closed off but the lack of heat didn't stop Ellen. She would sneak in and play until her fingers were frozen and blue with cold.

She became proficient enough to play the organ for the afternoon Dutch services held in her church. Her brother, Arnie, would go along, and during the preaching of the sermon, which was usually very long, they would entertain themselves by reading and telling stories.

She taught a boys' Sunday school class and accompanied the children's singing for programs. She joined a 4H club and won several trips to conventions in Lansing, Michigan and to the State Fair in Detroit, Michigan.

Ellen didn't live in a large city, but she was a city girl nonetheless. Her parents were well to do and enjoyed many comforts. Ellen adored her father and if he didn't outright spoil her, he certainly pampered her. Photographs of Ellen reveal a slender, stylish, good-looking, young woman of obvious intelligence and good breeding.

Henry may have been from the country, but he was no bumpkin. He cut a dashing figure - tall, dark and handsome. He was several years older than Ellen and after they met, they dated for four years. Once, during that time, Ellen jilted him and started dating someone else, mostly for spite, she admitted later. Her parents weren't happy about her new beau and her dad announced that if she kept dating him she would have to pay for her own tuition, should she go on to college.

Ellen eventually went back to Henry, her first love, but the fact she had hurt him must have bothered her, because she brought it up on her deathbed.

It was only one and one half miles from her childhood home in town to her new home, but it might as well have been a hundred, so great was the contrast between Ellen's leisurely, cultured and bountiful life in town and the life she would experience on the farm. Bountiful would take on a new meaning for her there.

"...Intreat me not to leave thee, or to return from following after thee: for whither thou goest, I will go; and where thou lodgest, I will lodge: thy people shall be my people and thy God, my God: Where thou diest, will I die, and there will I be buried: the Lord do so to me and more also if ought but death part thee and me." Ruth 1:16,17

"...stir up the gift of God, which is in thee by the putting on of hands."
II Timothy 1:6

If she had wanted, Ellen could have been a dynamo in whatever profession she chose. She had the intelligence, determination and energy to accomplish whatever she set out to do, but she had no aspirations outside of being a homemaker. Though she supported Henry's work on the farm, her place was in the home. She was "like a fruitful vine in the inner part of his {Henry's} house."[1]

Nothing in Ellen's life, growing up in a comfortable, well-to-do home in the city, could have prepared her for the stark reality of living on (and off) the land; still, she threw herself into her new life with determination and optimism, for she loved Henry with all her heart and was totally committed to their life together.

The farm is bleak in March. A grim austere landscape greeted Ellen in mid/late March as she and Henry returned from their honeymoon and began settling into their new home.

Looking out the kitchen window, on her first morning on the farm, she would have seen the sun rising to the east. Barren scraggy trees stood here and there in the yard. Sooty stale piles of snow were reminders of winter's frigid blast. Patches of green dotted the snow-covered pasture and a ring of water circled the frozen pond - hopeful signs that the bleak barrenness would not last forever. The pond wound lazily uphill to the woods, a scruffy, scraggly army of trees guarding the rear boundary.

She might have seen the cows - all six of them, relieved of their saggy udders, straggling out in a line to greet the first signs of spring, following their leader to seek what sustenance they could find in the grim wilderness of the pasture.

As she waited for Henry to return from his early milking for breakfast, her sense of excitement and exuberance shifted to a twinge of uncertainly and doubt, triggered perhaps by the foreboding scene framed in the kitchen window.

Suddenly she felt vulnerable, alone and unsure of

herself. What was she doing here? She knew nothing of farm life or being a farm wife. Her comfortable leisurely life back home, just one and a half miles away, seemed far away indeed.

The only farm she knew was her Grandpa and Grandma Battan's and that was not a working farm - just a cow for milking and a few hens for laying eggs. She had visited farms with her father because, during the depression, farmers often paid their store accounts with produce, milk, eggs and fruit, or sometimes, provided services for Benjamin. Ellen recalled being invited inside a farmhouse once and thinking how dirty and smelly it was. She vowed then that she would never be a farmwife when she got married.

Yet here she was in the kitchen, dressed in her new housedress and apron feeling lost and alone.

Suddenly a flash of red flew past the window. Ellen noticed a male cardinal perched on a limb in the yard, his shebird a few branches up. *A pair of cardinals,* she thought. *A pair, just like Henry and me.* The sight of them lifted her spirits. Henry would be home soon. He would make everything right. She loved him with all her heart. He was a farmer, so she would be his farmwife. *Well, a housewife who lives on the farm,* she thought. Somehow that sounded better.

Ellen started the coffee, set the sausages sizzling and whipped the pancake batter into a froth. Henry would soon be home. He would be hungry. She had better get busy fixing his breakfast.

Ellen's life on the farm had begun.

The variety of jobs facing her was mind-boggling.

First she needed to learn how to cook proper meals for a hardworking man like her Henry, who was up with the sun to milk the cows and whose work wasn't finished until the sun went down in the evening. Breakfast, dinner and supper with snacks mid-morning and mid-afternoon and one before bedtime. The noon meal, the largest meal of the day, called for meat, potatoes and all the trimmings.

Over time, Ellen mastered the art of cooking and baking. Seven-layer dinner, meat loaf, scalloped potatoes and baked beans, Russian Fluff casserole, pancakes and waffles, rice with raisins made in the double boiler, homemade applesauce, spaghetti, caramelized carrots, sweet corn and corn cut off the cob boiled in milk for Henry, canned peaches (Henry's favorite), headcheese, chicken with mashed potatoes and gravy, blackcaps, Johnny Cake (cornbread dipped in bacon grease and soaked in syrup) with side pork, strawberry shortcake, using her famous Dunlap strawberries, rhubarb and pineapple upside down cake and even homemade ice cream were some of her signature meals and favorite creations.

Her pies were almost too beautiful to disturb. She made fruit pies, lemon meringue and butterscotch cream pies, among others. Once a week she baked four loaves of bread. Henry always happened to be around when they came out of the oven, all aglow with their shiny buttered tops. She baked cinnamon rolls and delicious sugar doughnuts. The rolls were drizzled with frosting and the doughnuts, still warm from the frying pan, were shaken in a bag filled with sugar and cinnamon.

Ellen managed her food budget on a strict allowance. It helped some that much of their food came from the farm, like the raw warm non-pasteurized milk Henry brought home after milking. After sitting in the jars for a day or so, the butterfat or cream would rise to the top and could be used for whipping cream to top off a slice of apple pie. A butchered cow provided their meat. Ellen canned the meat until a freezer was purchased and the steaks, hamburger, ribs and roasts could be frozen. They enjoyed asparagus, cherries, apples and potatoes from the land's yield, but making do was still a challenge, especially when the children were born.

Ellen was never happier than when the shelves in her fruit cellar were lined with rows of canned fruits, vegetables and meat. She canned sweet cherries, sweet pickles, dill pickles, chunk pickles, jam, blackcaps, applesauce, tomato juice, over 100 cans of stewed tomatoes pickled peaches and regular peaches, one of Henry's favorite dishes. She always got 13 quarts of peaches from one bushel of fruit and was proud that she could peel a peach in one continuous strip, without lifting her paring knife.

She made jelly by placing the fruit, such as cherries or blackberries into a cheesecloth bag and letting the juice drip through into a pan. She then thickened the juice, poured it into jars and sealed it with a layer of paraffin over the top.

Ellen was a master at multitasking. Her chores were done within the rhythm of the day. She would peel the peaches, get them into the cooker and then, while they were boiling, she'd hang out a basket of clothes, mix up a batch of bread dough or pick and snip a pan of green beans from the garden.

Doing the laundry was perhaps the biggest challenge for Ellen, for it meant she had to use the scary ringer washing machine.

First she filled the tubs - the washtub with hot water and the rinse tub with cold water. When the washtub was filled and the detergent added, the agitator was activated with a crank. While the clothes were agitating, Ellen eyed the scary ringer, remembering stories she had read of women who had had terrible accidents with the moving roller - one woman had gotten her arm caught and another, her hair. This woman's scalp was torn off as her hair was pulled through the ringer. Ellen shuddered at the grizzly thought, vowing to be extra careful.

The basement was not Ellen's favorite place. Two small windows allowed some light, but it was still dark and dismal. The coal furnace dominated the room. When it was running, it rumbled and rattled like a dragon, spewing its heat through the registers upstairs. The coal cellar was in one corner. It had a door to the outside where the coal was shoveled down a ramp into the grim interior. Coal dust flew everywhere as the black briquettes tumbled down the ramp. Ellen could deal with the dust permeating the atmosphere in the basement but she disliked any unnecessary dirt upstairs (for that reason she insisted Henry keep his farm clothes and shoes down there). The fruit cellar took up another corner and in another, Henry had put up clotheslines in case of inclement weather.

The clothes sloshed around in the washer like riders in a tilt-a-whirl she had seen once at a county fair.

Ellen kept one eye on the dreaded ringer. When the clothes done, she took a deep breath and stifling her fears, picked up the end of a dripping pillowcase.

"Lord, help me," she whispered as she fed the case carefully through the rollers into the rinse tub. Then back through the ringer one more time after which, flat as a pancake, the case dropped with a thud into the waiting basket below.

Once all the clothes had been rinsed and wrung, Ellen took her clothes basket and clothespins and carried then up the basement stairs and outside to the clotheslines Henry had put up for her on the south side of the house. There she hung them out to dry, hoping it wouldn't rain and that no cars would ruin her clean clothes by raising dust on the dirt road that ran in front of the house.

On a crisp Monday morning in mid-April, Ellen had just pinned her last bed sheet onto the line when a little black-capped chickadee (she knew what chickadees were) came and perched on a branch overhead, trilling its little heart out.

"Oh you beautiful little creature," Ellen called. Something about that plump little bird lifted her spirits and gave her a burst of hope like the cardinals had done for her earlier.

She felt a deep longing within - it seemed to come from the very depths of her being, from her soul. It was an awakening to nature and the power of birds singing, trees budding, breezes blowing and clothes flapping in the wind. It was then she knew there was a power beyond all that she could see, smell, hear and feel.

She had learned about God in church and Sunday school and had publicly professed her faith when she was eighteen. She and Henry, in their wedding vows, had promised to make God the center of their home.

But now in a bird's song, she experienced the God of creation and revelation in her heart. God was in the bird's song, the budding of the trees, the cooling refreshing breeze and the tulips blooming by the side of the house. She didn't have to worry about her new life or feel lonely or isolated when Henry left her to do his chores about the farm. With God's help she could become the housewife she wanted to be for Henry's sake. She felt strangely moved - changed even. Ellen had experienced a moment out of time - a kairos moment.

    She lingered there awhile as the clothes flapped about her in the breeze. Before going inside, she eyed the dirt road that ran in front of the house. Wondering if God had time for such details, she lifted up a prayer. "Dear God, please don't let any cars come by..."

    Feeling refreshed, she picked up her empty basket and went inside.

    After the washing came the ironing. Ellen ironed everything - even the sheets and pillowcases. As she ironed she must have thought back to the time when she worked on Saturdays for a minister's wife, ironing and starching the sheets, the huge white tablecloths and the Dominie's shirts. Her arms got so tired from pushing the heavy iron around, she lasted only one year.

    There was no quitting now. Ellen, though a novice at being a housewife, would rise to the challenges facing her. She wanted to make Henry proud of her.

    The house on the hill had a basement, two bedrooms, a bathroom, a kitchen and dining room on the main floor and two small bedrooms and a landing upstairs. After the children were born, a living room was added. Every week, Ellen mopped and cleaned her floors, cleaned the windows and dusted and polished the furniture. She aimed to keep her house clean and free of the dirt and stench of the farm.

    Henry had his mid-morning and mid-afternoon snacks on the back stairway so he wouldn't track in the house with his farm shoes. In the evenings he left his farm clothes in the basement.

    When it was time for spring cleaning, Henry hauled the mattresses outside where they were beaten. Together they washed the walls and emptied and cleaned the cupboards.

    Spring was also the time for putting in the garden.

Henry tilled the soil, planted the seeds and weeded the young plants. Rows of onions, radishes, peas, tomatoes, squash, string beans, cucumbers and sweet corn grew up to the sun. Ellen's chores doubled with the picking, preparing, canning and freezing of the fruits and vegetables.

She grew nasturtiums, peonies, lilies, mums, snapdragons and roses in her flowerbeds. The roses were her favorites. She purchased them from the Jackson and Perkins catalogue and knew each one by name.

In the evenings, when Henry was reading in the living room, Ellen would sit with her basket, darning socks and mending clothes. She would knit or crochet sweaters, scarves and mittens and tat handkerchiefs and doilies. She was constantly busy. Did she rue the fact that she had very little time left over from her chores to play the upright piano Henry had bought her?

Ellen spent many hours at her electric sewing machine - another gift from Henry. She sewed clothes for herself and the children, when they came along. She was very resourceful where the children's wardrobes were concerned. Once she fashioned a snowsuit for Roger out of an old woolen overcoat. It was so heavy he could hardly walk in it, much less play! She made Marilyn a winter coat from one of her father, Benjamin's old woolen overcoats. Marilyn was a bit nonplussed to wear it to school and one day she was humiliated to find that another student had thrown it outside with the rubbish.

With determination, hard work and diligence, Ellen was fanning the flame of her gifts in her role of housewife. She wanted Henry to be proud of her. And he was.

"Whoso findeth a wife findeth a good thing, and obtaineth favor of the Lord." Proverbs 18:22

Homemaking was Ellen's highest excellence and although she never set foot in the barn, she encouraged Henry's work on the farm and supported his endeavors wholeheartedly.

Since Henry worked for his father Andrew, he earned only a share of the profits. Every Saturday evening they would settle up and Henry would come home with his earnings for the week. Ellen may not have been directly involved with Henry's work, but she was certainly affected by the farm's successes or failures.

Unlike Ellen, Henry was accustomed to farm life. After all, he had grown up on the farm and had worked alongside his father all his life. Now, although he was married, his duties didn't change much - milking and feeding the cows and calves, tilling, plowing and seeding the fields, picking asparagus, threshing, filling silo, potato digging and corn shredding. The farm now included cherry orchards and a large field of beans, which required tending and picking. Fences around the pastures needed to be built and repaired.

One of the most exciting times on the farm was threshing day, the modern term for what was once called thrashing, so called because back then, farmers used "flails" to beat the wheat and separate the grain from the stalk.

Back then, the local farmers, including Andrew and Henry, pooled their time and equipment and traveled around from farm to farm helping each other thresh and harvest the wheat.

Early in the morning, the sounds of the caravan of tractors, horses and threshing equipment could be heard coming up the road. Leading the procession was the tractor pulling the threshing machine. Following behind were other tractors - Farmalls, John Deeres and an old Silver King, all spouting exhaust. Behind the tractors came the teams of horses pulling wagons. Their drivers stood on the wagons, holding the reins. It was a grand sight indeed.

The threshing machine was set in place near the granary where the grain would be stored. Its big spout was positioned so the straw would blow into the barn. Then the farmers would be assigned their jobs.

Those sent to the fields forked the bundles of grain onto the wagons. One person would drive the team of horses and another would be atop the wagon arranging the bundles in neat piles. There were usually three teams of horses in the field and when each wagon was full, the driver would pull it to the threshing machine where the bundles would be forked into the machine. The owner of the threshing machine would stand on top of his machine and watch that the bundles weren't fed in too fast. He got very angry if the machine jammed. Two farmers then carried the bags of grain from the machine and dumped them into the granary bins. Henry had the dirtiest job. He stood in the straw shed and forked the straw around as it was blown into the shed. When he emerged, his face was pitch black except for his eyes, which were protected by goggles.

The men stopped for brief morning and afternoon snacks but twelve o'clock was dinnertime. And what a feast it was!

After washing off some of the soot and grime outdoors, they took their places at the dining room table in Andrew and Jane's house. Andrew offered a prayer and they dug in.

For days, Jane and Ellen had been busy preparing food. All morning they worked setting up the table and getting the food ready to serve. There were platters of meat, bowls of mashed potatoes and boats of gravy. There were string beans, carrots and peas, squash and homemade applesauce. Slices of bread, still warm from the oven, were slathered with freshly churned butter and homemade jellies and jams. Then came the pies served with ice cream or whipping cream. There was a choice of cherry, apple, lemon meringue or blackberry.

As they ate, the farmers caught up on all the latest happenings around the countryside. Many a story was spun around the table and laughter and good humor helped to alleviate aching muscles and stiff joints. After dinner, while the women cleared the table and washed and dried the dishes, the men went back to work to finish up. Usually threshing was a one-day affair and the farmers would stay as long as necessary, sometimes after sundown, to complete the job. Then they were gone and all was quiet once again.

While the vulnerabilities of living and working on the land must have become more apparent to Henry with a wife and the anticipation of children to feed and tend, Ellen, new to the farm, was learning about eking out a living on the land.

A sick cow could contaminate the milk and ruin an entire batch of milk. Too little rain and the newly planted seeds could suffocate; too much and they would wash away. A windstorm could destroy an entire cherry crop. To make matters worse, the cherries would have to be picked and dumped to insure the success of next year's crop.

Though Henry was used to the rigors of farm life, Ellen developed an amazing capacity to comfort and calm Henry's fears in the face of adversity. Though they leaned on each other and were committed to their life together no matter what the odds, it was often Ellen who propped up Henry's deflated spirits with the words that would become her mantra – "God will provide."

Her role of helpmeet was every bit as challenging as that

of homemaker. It taught her the lesson that Henry had learned from years of working the land - in the end, all is of God.

"Lord, I have loved the habitation of thy house, and the place thine glory dwelleth." Psalm 26:8

Henry and Ellen's faith was honed on the farm. Though they had both been raised in God-fearing, church-going families, the faith of their youth would be tested and tried by eking out a living on the land. Like a muscle, it would be exercised by daily stretching and would grow as strong as the rocks turned over by the plow in the field; their trust in God as sure as the sun that rose and set daily over their heads; their walk with God as straight and narrow as the furrows formed by the plow Henry held as he walked back and forth across the fields behind his workhorses, Maud and Daize.

Ellen had joined Henry's church, which they attended twice every Sunday. Henry served on the consistory and Ellen was a member of a ladies' Bible study, often serving as president. Once when their church was without a pastor, she was asked to lead the Bible study. Once a year she attended Missionary Union, an all-day event. She played the organ for the worship services, sang in a double trio and both she and Henry sang in the choir. Ellen's alto voice blended beautifully with Henry's rich tenor and they often sang duets for church and community events.

They belonged to the Gideon's International organization. While Henry visited churches and schools to distribute New Testaments to children, Ellen was a member of the Women's Auxiliary. Soon Henry was getting requests "to exhort" on behalf of the Gideon's. Larry Woiwode, in

What I Think I Did, explains that exhorting is a Presbyterian euphemism for what happens when a person who is not a pastor or "teaching elder" is asked to speak. [2]

In order to gain confidence in exhortation, Henry attended Toastmasters, an organization which specialized in public speaking.

Henry and Ellen attended programs at Maranatha Bible Conference in Muskegon, Michigan and spent a week at Winona Lake Bible Conference, in Indiana, every summer.

Still, in spite of their church involvement and ecumenical experiences, important as they were, Henry and Ellen honed their faith and spiritual life at home on the farm.

Henry, like Joshua of old, committed his family to the Lord. Morning devotions helped gird him for the rigors of the day while prayer before and after the noon and evening meals became a routine. Scripture was read before the closing prayer. Henry was well and widely read, but along with the book of history or poetry he was reading, there was always a bible by his recliner and a book written by one of the spiritual giants he had come to love and revere: Charles Hadden Spurgeon, Billy Graham, Dr. Harry Ironsides, Donald G. Barnhouse, Dwight L. Moody and his favorite, the old country preacher, Dr. Vance Havner.

Henry spent most of his waking hours outside where he became close to nature and to God. He would have agreed with Dr. Havner's view of the country:

"I thank God that I grew up in the country, 'far from the madding crowd's ignoble strife.' God made the country and man made the town - and you can certainly see the difference! A country boy may learn city ways but a city boy cannot learn country ways - you have to be born and grow up in the country to be natural. Someone said that city people and country folks are just ignorant on different subjects." [3]

While guiding the plow in the fields behind Maud and Daize, Henry listened to the birds chirping and singing. He watched the killdeer gliding to and fro on its spindly stick-like legs. The hawks hovered high over the maple tree as he snapped the tall green asparagus stalks. He rose with the sun and watched it rise over the eastern horizon, arc across the sky and plunge into the western hills, an orange ball of fire, at day's end.

He knew numerous birdcalls and songs and could predict the weather by watching the sky and the cloud formations. He was a walking Farmer's Almanac. "That's a September sky," he would say, looking up at the clouds. "There's a red sky tonight. We should get rain tomorrow." "Rain before 7 will end by 11."

As he went about his chores, Scripture verses he had read and memorized were internalized until they sank into his soul and became planted there like fertile seeds. Like the seeds he planted, Henry became an apple tree himself planted by rivers of water, bearing its yield in season, with leaves that would never wither and fruit that would never be damaged with wind blight. [4]

Nature was his university. If wisdom comes by seeing the world from God's point of view, Henry became wise as he milked the cows, harvested the corn, and mended the fences.

Nature was as much a sanctuary for him during the week as church was on Sunday. He came to know his heavenly Father through creation and meditation as well as through Scripture reading and prayer. To Henry, worship was not a part of life experienced on Sunday in church - it *was* his life.

"Because that which may be known of God is manifest in them; for God hath shewed it unto them. For the invisible things of him from the creation of the world are clearly seen, being understood by the things that are made, even his eternal power and Godhead; so that they are without excuse." Romans 1:19,20

Ellen had encountered her Lord when she was hanging out clothes during her first days on the farm. That experience had helped her overcome her initial fears and doubts about being a housewife on the farm and given her a peace that had remained deep in her soul.

That experience helped to lift her above the daily grind of life, to see beyond the physical to the spiritual - to know the spiritual *in* the physical. Whenever the vulnerabilities of farm life overwhelmed and engulfed her, she would dig deep into the reservoir of that initial encounter with God in nature, when His attributes were revealed to her.

As she went about her daily chores, especially when she was outside hanging up the clothes or working in her garden or her flowerbeds, the truths contained in her daily Scripture reading became real to her and their mysteries unfolded in her heart.

She came to understand that there is more to life than what one can see, touch, taste or feel - more than what one can sense. Though she realized the sacredness of nature, she was no pantheist. Her feeling of reverence and awe at a bird's song or a beautiful sunset were firmly grounded in the belief that the God of Creation was also the God of Scripture. He was revealed in both.

For Ellen, like Henry, creation was a means to help her see God and worship Him, "in the beauty of His holiness."

During her life on the farm, Ellen often met her Lord in

the garden as she lovingly tended her roses, cut them, trimmed them back and then fashioned them into fragrant bouquets.

> "I come to the garden alone,
> While the dew is still on the roses.
> And the voice I hear falling on my ear,
> The Son of God discloses.
>
> And He walks with me and he talks with me
> And he tells me I am His own.
> And the joy we share as we tarry there,
> None other can ever know." (C. Austin Miles) [5]

No matter that the composer, C. Austin Miles, was writing about the first Easter morning and the garden where Jesus was buried. It was here, we are told, Mary Magdalene came alone very early, "while the dew was still on the roses." When Jesus first spoke to her, she thought He was the gardener, but when He called her by name, she recognized His voice. Imagine Mary's feelings at that moment when Jesus called her name. She had seen her Lord die on the cross. She was coming now to anoint His dead body with spices. But now He was standing before her and talking to her. He was alive! At first she was startled, but when she recognized her Lord, imagine her joy!

Mary's experience is relived by every person who confronts the risen Christ and realizes His presence in the routine of daily life. [6]

One can imagine Ellen communing with her Lord when life came at her hard. As Jacob of old lifted up the stone, on which he had rested, as an altar to God, so Ellen came to the garden, lifted up her problems and struggles and laid them on the altar. There, at the altar, she sought divine help and solace and offered up her will to her God. Throughout her lifetime, one experience at a time, she erected a pile of stones - a cairn, a stairway to heaven, an altar, bridging the gap between herself and God.

"Ellen."

"Oh, my Lord, is it You?"

"Yes, I am here. Why are you crying my dear one?"

"Oh, my Lord," she wailed, "the cherry crop has been ruined by the wind. Oh, I do not know what to do. If Henry cannot pick the cherries we will not have the money we need to pay our bills. We were counting on that money."

Her voice broke off into a sob.

"Ellen." The voice was sweet and so, so gentle. "Ellen. When you first found me here on the farm, did I not promise to take care of you?"

"Yes, Lord, but I did not realize the way would be so hard. Oh, my Lord, not only is the entire crop ruined, but Henry has to pay to have the cherries picked, otherwise next year's crop will be ruined. Oh, my Lord, what are we to do?"

She sank to the ground, sobs wracking her body.

"Ellen, Ellen - "did I promise that the way would always be easy? Did I promise you a rose garden?"

In spite of her woes, the hint of a smile wafted to her lips.

"No, my Lord. But I am so frightened and I need to be strong for Henry. Please, my Lord, help me. It's hard to be strong when I'm afraid myself. I don't know how we will manage."

"Ellen. Remember, what I told you. 'If ye abide in me, and my words abide in you, ye shall ask what ye will, and it shall be done unto you.' Now, if you had a wish, what would it be?"

Ellen was quiet for a time. Then, with some hesitation, she ventured, "Oh, I wish this had never happened! I wish the cherries had never been ruined. Would it be possible, oh, if it please my Lord, is there any way You could make the cherries, well," it sounded so silly, what she was asking, "could you undo the wind damage? Henry is beside himself with worry. He wants so badly to provide for me. If it please, my Lord, I remember the story in the bible, how you commanded the wind and the waves and, at your word, they were still. Could you, oh my Lord, could you, do that for us?"

"My dear Ellen. Even if I did undo the damage, are you certain this is what you would wish for?"

Ellen pondered the question. "If you put it that way, my Lord, I suppose that if we, well, if we just had enough money, it wouldn't matter if the cherries were ruined, would it?" It sounded so mercenary, trivial even, but Ellen kept on. "Could, could you make that possible? My Lord, could you just provide us with enough money to buy food and other things we need?"

"Is that your wish then - money?"

Ellen realized her Lord was putting her faith to the test.

"No, I guess not." She was quiet for a time.

"This is my wish my Lord - that You would comfort Henry and give him the strength to go on in spite of losing his cherries. He cannot survive without hope and he worries so about taking care of me. Yes, that is my wish - to give Henry peace and make him strong."

He smiled.

"Your wish is granted my dear Ellen. It is written: 'But they that wait upon the Lord shall renew their strength; they shall mount up with wings as eagles; they shall run, and not be weary; and they shall walk, and not faint.' And, now a wish for yourself?"

"Nothing for myself, my Lord. It is enough to be here with You in the garden."

Again He smiled upon her.

"You have chosen well my child. Go with my blessing: 'That he would grant you, according to the riches of his glory, to be strengthened with might by his Spirit in the inner {being...}'"

Then He was gone.

Ellen remained in the garden for a time, savoring the moments with her Lord. Something stirred deep within her - she felt altered, transformed. Her eyes filled with tears but they were tears of wonderment and joy. Gently she wiped her eyes and went in to fix supper for Henry.

(Scripture texts used in this section are from John 15:7, Isaiah 40:31, and Ephesians 3:16)

"And, why take ye thought for raiment? Consider the lilies of the field, how they grow; they toil not, neither do they spin: And yet I say unto you, That even Solomon in all his glory was not arrayed like one of these." Matthew 6:28,29

Ellen may have been a housewife living on a farm, but she never thought of herself as *just* a housewife. That distinction became clear not only when she went about her chores, but also when she had some time for herself.

She turned housework into an aesthetic adventure. She took pride in ironing the sheets and pillowcases. A batch of strawberry jam, thirteen jars of canned peaches, rows of tomato juice, a pan of snipped beans and a freshly baked blackberry pie were works of art for Ellen. She hummed and sang as she hung out the clothes. Her presence and energy transformed the house on the hill into a home filled with a hustle and bustle of activity, aromas of fragrant bouquets, loaves of bread baking and suppers on the stove.

She tended her flowers with tender loving care. She cut and fashioned bouquets, which filled the house with an ambience of beauty and fragrance.

She loved going to nearby Stony Lake or Lake Michigan for a few hours whenever she had a break from her chores. She loved swimming her vintage sidestroke and the feel of sand between her toes.

She and Henry would take rides in the country just to get away from the farm for an hour or two. Some of their favorite outings were to a roadside park north of Ludington, Michigan, Gull Landing in Pentwater, Michigan or a ride to the lake to see the sunset.

Their outings became somewhat more challenging after the children were born, with nine people packed into the car - four in the front seat and five wedged into the back. It was crowded and noisy with the children in the back fighting for window seats and asking to stop along the way. No wonder Ellen often suffered from migraine headaches on these family outings.

Occasionally the family would take a vacation with Ellen's parents, Benjamin and Winnie. How Ellen must have loved getting away for a few days and eating out, even though eating out for Ellen meant packing picnics for everyone.

Henry had bought her a piano for an anniversary gift and Ellen loved sitting at the keyboard whenever she had a chance. She maintained her proficiency on the organ also and played for worship services at their church.

Her handiwork was both practical and aesthetic. She knit and crocheted sweaters, mittens, scarves and afghans, tatted handkerchiefs and doilies, did embroidery and candle wicking on tablecloths and later on created over 75 quilts for her children, grandchildren and great grandchildren - each one a work of beauty and a visual testimony to her artistry.

When time permitted, she loved reading books and discussing ideas and current issues. Her opinions were always founded on the bible and though she would listen to varying opinions and viewpoints, she was firm on what the bible taught.

Ellen wholeheartedly accepted her role as Henry's wife and helpmeet, yet she must have had dreams and ideas just bursting to be free. She was intelligent, cultured, determined and creative. She had the capacity to do anything she chose to do; yet, there was very little time in her day to pursue anything for herself. When life was hard and she and Henry struggled just to make ends meet, she must have wondered if her dreams, or the dreams she had for her children, would ever find fulfillment. Yet, she never flinched in fulfilling God's purpose for her as homemaker and helpmeet in the house on the hill.

"Consider the lilies..."

"Lo, children are an heritage of the Lord; and the fruit of the womb is his reward. As arrows are in the hand of a mighty man; so are children of the youth. Happy is the man that hath his quiver full of them..." Psalm 127: 3-5

"He maketh the barren woman to keep house, and to be a joyful mother of children. Praise the Lord." Psalm 113:9

Henry and Ellen had been married only a year when their first child was born. Marilyn Kay came into their lives on April 7, 1937.

As they tended their fields and garden, so they tended their first baby lovingly and committed her to the Lord.

How they fussed and cooed over their precious little bundle of joy! Ellen was still adjusting to her role of housewife and now her life was wonderfully stretched to include the duties of a mother - nursing the baby, changing and washing diapers, going for buggy rides in the fresh air, sewing baby clothes and rocking her baby to sleep at night.

Henry, the proud papa, beamed at this miracle of life and during his morning snack time, earned a smile by tickling his baby girl under the chin.

Henry and Ellen believed that children were a blessing from God and on a Sunday in mid-April they presented their first-born to the Lord. Nestled inside a white crocheted blanket was baby Marilyn, dressed in a beautiful white knitted dress and bonnet, all lovingly made by Ellen for this special occasion.

They spoke their vows at the baptismal font, promising to raise their child in a Christian home. Marilyn was then baptized into the name of the Father and the Son and the Holy Spirit. She cooed as the drops of water ran down her forehead into her eyes.

Like Hannah of old, they acknowledged their child was a gift of God and was entrusted to their care and spiritual nurture.

Henry and Ellen had seven children in all, three sons and four daughters, each one loved and welcomed into their family and baptized into the family of God. Roger Wendell was born on July 2, 1938, Judith Mae, on Sept. 16, 1939, Wendell Royce was born on May 26, 1941, Joan Ellen on

Aug. 15, 1942, Janet Lynne on Nov. 10, 1944 and Randall Henry, the youngest, in March, 1947.

These dates reveal a somewhat startling fact: from July, 1936, just four months after starting life together on the farm, until March, 1947 – an eleven-year span, except for one year, 1945, Ellen was either pregnant or giving birth to a new born.

With each addition to their family however, the chores and challenges increased. Now a mother and a housewife, Ellen shifted into high gear. She washed and ironed twice a week, changing five beds each week. She had nine hungry mouths to feed on a weekly allowance of $20.00. One batch of bread or cinnamon rolls could disappear in one sitting! At lunchtime she stood in the kitchen flipping pancakes, forever, it seemed, until the children were full and she could sit down to eat a couple for herself.

She would finish the breakfast dishes, make a coffeecake and prepare the meat and potatoes for the noon meal and there would be Henry and the children, on the back stairs, ready for their morning snack. The noon meal was the main meal of the day. It consisted of meat, potatoes, gravy, vegetables, bread or rolls and a dessert and required a great deal of preparation. Then, after the table was cleared and the dishes washed and wiped, it was time to think about the mid-afternoon snack and supper.

In between preparing the meals, she washed, hung out clothes and ironed, canned and froze fruits and vegetables, dusted, weeded her flowerbed, cut and arranged flowers, picked and prepared vegetables from the garden, plucked plump berries from the blackcap bushes, sewed and mended clothes, got groceries and ran errands, washed children's hair, gave them baths and saw to it that each had the proper medical and dental care.

In addition to the challenges of her routine chores, there was the occasional emergency or crisis and, with seven children, there were accidents just waiting to happen.

Joan and Janet, on two different occasions, had fingers pinched in the car door and had to be taken to the emergency room. One morning Wendell knocked himself out cold when he tripped over his lunch pail while running out to Aunt Lena's car. Aunt Lena worked at the grocery store in New Era and drove the children to school each morning. The rest of the children, waiting in the car, watched him crumple in a huddled heap in the yard. They thought he was dead.

Another time, Henry and Ellen were enjoying an evening away at Maranatha Bible Conference in Muskegon when they were called out of their program to discover that Janet had broken her arm. The younger children, left at home in charge of the older siblings, had organized a swing-jumping contest. Janet won but broke her arm in the process. And these were just a few.

To complicate matters, Henry and Ellen had no insurance, so the medical bills had to come from an already stretched budget.

The children spent much time outdoors. When she had the time, Ellen would take them on walks to the woods or have picnics outside. In the spring and summer, they earned money by picking asparagus, cherries and beans. Oftentimes Henry worked alongside them and brought them morning and afternoon snacks, which Ellen prepared. Around the house they picked strawberries, blackcaps and helped Ellen in her garden.

In the summer, Jane's sister, Lene and her husband, John would visit from Chicago. The children loved it when they came. Uncle John always had candy in his pocket and a twinkle in his eye.

There were games of Hide and Go Seek, Kick the Can, Red Rover and baseball in the yard. All was fine until a fly ball smashed one of Grandma Jane's windows. After that the children were banished to the pasture to play ball among the cow pies.

When the chores were done, the family would go on beach outings to Stony Lake and Lake Michigan.

Henry included the children in the farm chores, whenever he could. He bought little milk pails for the boys so they could learn to milk the cows, just as he had learned alongside his father, though rousing them out of bed for the early milking was a chore in itself. The children loved taking turns riding the workhorses, Maud and Daize. How Henry must have enjoyed instilling in his children a love of nature by teaching them birdcalls and pointing out cloud formations in the sky as he walked back and forth across the fields behind the horses.

After meals there were lively family discussions around the dining room table. It was always a highly charged atmosphere and a challenge to get one's views "on the table." Once, Roger became so animated he picked up a jam jar and heaved it across the table to make his point.

One day a large box postmarked from the Schwinn Bicycle Co., came in the mail. The box was addressed to Judith VanGunst and inside was a brand new 10-speed bicycle. Judi had entered a contest posted on the back of a cereal box. Contestants were invited to enter suggestions for the name of a new line of 10-speed bikes. She entered the name, "The Blue Flyer," which won first place and a brand new bike.

Aunt Lena, next door, taught the children piano lessons. She taught on a rather loose schedule and when she announced that she was available to give a lesson, there was always a scramble to decide whose turn it was. The chosen one – the sacrificial lamb, would head for the piano to do some quick cramming.

Though the boys mostly helped Henry with the farm duties, they did help Ellen too, especially on washdays. They emptied the wash and rinse tubs of water into pails and dumped them outside.

The girls helped Ellen in the house. They learned to iron, set and clear the table at meal times, wash and dry the dishes and help with the cleaning. In the summers the girls and Henry would go blackberry picking with Grandma Jane and her sister, Lene, who was visiting from Chicago. It was a study in contrasts. The girls wore shorts and short sleeved shirts in order to get a tan while the elderly ladies wore wide-brimmed hats, long sleeved shirts and long skirts to avoid the sun and the mosquitoes. The berries they brought home ended up in a delicious blackberry pie.

The children loved playing pranks on each other. Once, when Roger and Wendell were sleeping outside in their little pup tent, the girls came by to scare them. Roger and Wendell, sure there was a bear outside their tent, ran to the house, much to the merriment of everyone.

It was a busy household. There just were not enough hours in the day to do everything Ellen needed to do. How she must have wished that she had the time to go for walks with her children, as she had done in the beginning, when there were just one or two. How she must have wished for time to read them stories and sit with each one individually, but that became impossible to do.

There were happy times, but, with seven lively children, there were bound to be times of discord and stress also.

Roger remembered one instance, when on a family

outing, Ellen, in tears, pulled him aside.

"Roger, the younger children are playing ball and they're arguing over whose turn it is to bat. Your father is so upset with them. I know he's worrying about the lack of rain for his corn and he just doesn't have the patience right now. Can you help please? I want so much for this picnic to be a happy time."

There had to have been many such times when Ellen's intentions for a pleasant family outing went awry.

As much as she and Henry loved their children and considered them a blessing from God, a large family had its challenges.

Henry's share of the profits, hardly enough for the two of them, just wasn't enough for a family of nine. Ellen pleaded with Henry to ask Andrew for a larger percentage and it was increased slightly but it still was not sufficient. In desperation, Ellen was forced to ask her father, Benjamin, for help. Without his assistance and a charge account at the grocery store, which she used quite liberally, they would not have been able to make ends meet.

And, so they eked out a living on the farm. The vulnerabilities of life loomed large at times and became overwhelming. Again, we can imagine Ellen communing with her Lord.

"I come to the garden..."

"He speaks and the sound of His voice
Is so sweet, the birds hush their singing,
And the melody that He gave to me,
Within my heart is ringing.

And he walks with me and he talks with me,

And He tells me I am His own.
And the joy we share as we tarry there,
None other has ever known." (C. Austin Miles) [7]

"Ellen... Ellen, why are you crying?"
"Oh, my Lord, it is You. I am so worried. Janet has broken her arm and we have no insurance. We had to use our next month's grocery money to pay the doctor and the hospital bills!"
"Ellen." The voice was sweet and gentle. "Therefore I say to you, Take no thought for your life, what ye shall eat, or what ye shall drink; nor yet for your body, what ye shall put on. Is not the life more than meat and the body than raiment?"
"Yes, my Lord, but it is not for myself that I am worried. It is for my precious children. They need food and shoes and clothes for school and...please, my Lord, help me. Sometimes I don't know how we will get along. There just isn't enough money to buy the things they need."
"Ellen, my dear Ellen. 'Behold the fowls of the air: for they sow not, neither do they reap, nor gather into barns; yet your heavenly Father feedeth them. Are ye not much better than they?'"
It was quiet in the garden.
Then, "My dear, please stop worrying. 'Which of you by thought can add one cubit unto his stature? And why take ye thought for raiment? Consider the lilies of the field, how they grow; they toil not, neither do they spin: And yet I say into you, That even Solomon in all his glory was not arrayed like one of these... do you worry about clothes? See how the lilies of the field grow. They do not labor or spin. Yet I tell you that Solomon in all his glory was not arrayed like one of these. Wherefore, if God so clothe the

grass of the field, which today is, and tomorrow is cast into the oven, shall he not much more clothe you {Ellen}, O ye of little faith?'"

"Oh, my Lord. I want to believe. Please help me."

"It is written: 'But seek ye first the kingdom of God, and his righteousness; and all these things shall be added unto you. Take therefore no thought for the morrow: for the morrow shall take thought for the things of itself...'"

"My Lord, I am ashamed of myself for doubting. Sometimes, I think we need a miracle around here."

God smiled. "No matter. Miracles are what I'm good at. Now go in peace. 'Your faith has saved you.'"

And then, He was gone.

Ellen finished cutting her flowers, thinking over what her Lord had told her. Then, feeling strangely steadfast and humbled, she went inside to fashion a bouquet and finish her ironing.

(Scripture passages used in this section are from Matthew 6:25 – 34)

"I will lift up mine eyes unto the hills, from whence cometh my help. My help cometh from the Lord, which made heaven and earth." Psalm 121:1,2

Henry and Ellen had a screened-in front porch where they loved to sit and look out over the countryside. It was a small, cozy room, comfortable for two and with a little squeezing, it could accommodate four. Here they communed with nature, tired, but happy and contented after a hard day's work. They watched the birds, enjoyed the cool breeze, listened to the crickets singing and the frogs croaking. They watched the sun set over the western horizon. Henry claimed that he could see all the way out to Lake Michigan on a clear day.

Over the years, the porch came to be a refuge and a shelter for them - a place where they could come apart from the cares of the day and find rest. Perhaps, gazing outwards helped take their minds off their problems, while gazing upwards gave them a renewed perspective.

"For I reckon that the sufferings of this present time are not worthy to be compared with the glory which shall be revealed in us." Romans 8:18

How wonderful it would have been for Ellen if her in-laws, Henry's parents, Andrew and Jane, had been welcoming and supportive of her, a newcomer and novice to the farm and farm life, but whatever the reason, there was disharmony and tension from the beginning, with Henry caught in the middle, torn between his wife and family and his parents.

On his behalf, Andrew had overcome great odds and experienced much suffering in his life. He owned the farm and Henry worked for him. He certainly had a right to run the farm however he wished.

But how different it would have been for Ellen if she and Jane and sister-in-law, Lena, could have had a cup of coffee together now and then, shared recipes or had a friendly chat over the fence. How comforting to have had a friend or confidante with whom to share the challenges of farm life and rearing children.

Life was so lonely for Ellen at times that she walked a mile and a half to town to see her parents.

The loneliness and isolation were hard enough, but there were times, at family gatherings, when Ellen was shunned and ostracized by Henry's family. Once, at a family birthday party, Ellen left their house crying, because no one would talk to her.

Andrew, Jane and Lena seemed to feel quite comfortable interfering in Henry and Ellen's private domestic affairs.

Once after Henry had been sick, Jane and Lena, without consulting Ellen, took it upon themselves to call an ambulance to take Henry to the hospital.

In the fall of 1944, just after baby Janet was born, Henry was diagnosed with rheumatic fever. He was sick and in bed for many months. Now, added to her myriad household jobs, gardening chores, tending five children and a newborn baby, Ellen tended her beloved Henry and nursed him back to health.

How wonderful it would have been for her if her in-laws had helped her out and been supportive of her plight.

Sometimes life just seemed unfair. Seeking to earn a little extra cash for their family, Henry asked Andrew if he and Ellen could have an asparagus field of their own. They would till the soil, plant, weed and harvest the crop and in return, would receive all the profits.

With Andrew's verbal agreement, they set forth on their project. Picture them together, toiling in the fields, mixing little mustard seeds of faith in with the seedlings and praying for rain and a bountiful crop. At harvest time, the children worked along with them, walking up and down the rows, snapping off the tall green stalks and placing them in their baskets. Imagine Henry and Ellen, giddy with talk and plans for what they would do with a little extra money. After placing 10% into their tithing jar and paying off their grocery bill, they would buy a new bed for Randy, a new pair of shoes for Janet, a new coat for Joan, new winter jackets for Wendell and Roger and new dresses for Judith and Marilyn. If there was a little left over, oh joy! -

perhaps a new tie for Henry or a new hat for Ellen.

Then, oh anguish! Imagine their stunned disbelief when Andrew announced, after the asparagus harvest was over, that they had misunderstood the arrangement. He had never promised them all of the profits. They would receive their regular one-third share, a pittance of what they had anticipated. Oh the bitter disappointment! Oh the pain of what could have been!

Henry, a meek man by nature, was not inclined to confront his father over farm issues and though Ellen might have fought for what she thought was rightfully theirs, she respected Henry's decision and swallowed her bitter disappointment for his sake. There was nothing to do but to get on with earning a living. They didn't have time to waste feeling sorry for themselves. There were dishes waiting to be washed and cows waiting to be milked. They turned their hurts over to the Lord and went on with their lives.

Did her in-laws disapprove of her because she had jilted Henry earlier on in their courtship? Was it because she came from a well-to-do family in the city? Or was it because Ellen never thought of herself as *just* a farmwife, that they disparaged her. Perhaps Andrew resented her for meddling in his and Henry's business, blaming her for Henry's request that his share of the profits be increased from one fourth to one third. Perhaps they mistook her love of beauty, culture and sense of refinement as a better-than-thou attitude.

Whatever the reason, Ellen went on with the business of tending her family and creating a home. Her work kept her focused and centered and provided an outlet for her hurt feelings. Playing the piano and singing duets with Henry, knitting and embroidery and working in her flowerbeds brought healing to her soul. It helped to bring her hurts and disappointments to the Lord.

"I come to the garden alone..."

"I'd stay in the garden with Him
Though the night around me be falling.
But He bids me go; through the voice of woe,
His voice to me is calling."

And, He walks with me and He talks with me,
And He tells me I am His own.
And the joys we share as we tarry there,
None other has ever known. (C. Austin Miles) [8]

"Ellen."
"Oh, my Lord. Woe is me! Andrew promised Henry we could have our own asparagus patch and..."
"Ellen. I know."
"My Lord. You know what happened? Oh, we worked so hard. But, but, then my Lord - you, you know what happened. How unfair it was, for Andrew..."
"Ellen. I know."
"But, but..."
"Ellen, my dear Ellen. 'When He comes, He will convict the world of guilt in regard to sin and righteousness and judgment...' That is no concern of yours."
"But, my Lord, it was so unfair..."
"Ellen." The voice was sweet and gentle, but firm. "Ellen, my child, are you perfect then? Have *you* never hurt anyone? Have you never acted unfairly? It is written: '...for wherein thou judgest another, thou condemnest thyself; for thou that judgest doest the same things.' And

remember this: '... if ye forgive men their trespasses, your heavenly Father will also forgive you: But if ye forgive not men their trespasses, neither will your Father forgive your trespasses.'"

Ellen was quiet, her shortcomings washing over her like a flood. "Oh, my Lord, yes, I have sinned. I know that I have bad thoughts about Andrew and Jane sometimes, yes, and Lena too. I have not been as friendly to them as I could have been, because, my Lord, you see..."

"Ellen."

It was quiet in the garden.

"Oh, my Lord, my sins are many, I know. I pray that you will forgive me."

"It is written: 'And when ye stand praying, forgive, if ye have ought against any: that your Father also which is in heaven may forgive you your trespasses.'"

"Yes, my Lord. It is so hard to be good. Please help me."

"Ellen, remember what I told my disciples before I ascended to my Father in heaven: 'But the Comforter, which is the Holy Ghost, whom the Father will send in my name, he shall teach you all things, and bring all things to your remembrance, whatsoever I have said unto you.'"

"Oh, Lord, please stay with me awhile. I love it here in the garden with you. I have so much to learn. Please, could you stay a little longer?"

"Ellen. You have work to do. Remember, 'And ye now therefore have sorrow: but I will see you again, and your heart shall rejoice, and your joy no man taketh from you.' Now go in peace."

And He was gone. Or was He?

Ellen felt a fluttering within, like a brace of birds longing to be free. Free! Oh, how she longed to be free.

Free from the woes that beset them on the farm. Free from the lack of money, free from the dreaded windblight, free from sick cows and contaminated milk, free from lack of rain and parched earth, free from accidents, just waiting to happen. Free! Free! Free!

The flutterings increased until, like a wave, her fears rose up inside and nearly overwhelmed her. She could scarcely breathe. She thought her heart would burst. Then, with a sudden surge, the wave of flutterings burst forth and like a bird on the wing her soul felt light and free. As she stood in stunned relief, a stab of joy pierced her soul. In spite of everything, joy! It was just as her Lord had promised! She heard His words once again.

"...but I will see you again and your heart shall rejoice..."

Feeling lighthearted and refreshed, Ellen finished picking the row of beans and then took them inside to snip and wash for supper.

(Scripture verses in this section are from Romans 2:1, Matthew 6:14,15, Mark 11:25, John 14:26 and John 16:22)

"...if ye had faith as a grain of mustard seed, ye might say unto this sycamine tree, 'Be thou plucked up by the root and by thou planted in the sea; and it should obey you." Luke 17:6

Henry and Ellen's faith was honed on the farm. It has been said, "when faithfulness is most difficult, it is most necessary." Life was difficult for them, because, in living on the land, they were vulnerable in so many ways.

They were both brought up in God fearing homes. Bible reading and prayer were their spiritual bread and butter, a sure foundation for the many challenges and difficulties they would face.

Their faith got stronger as the years went by. Like a trainer strengthens a muscle through exercise so God strengthened their faith by stretching and exercising it.

Each time they faced a hardship, they would take it to the Lord in prayer, then trusting in His promises, they forged ahead with their work.

When the cherries were ruined by a windstorm, not only would there not be a cherry crop that year, but workers would have to be paid to pick and dump the fruit, otherwise the next year's crop would not come in.

Her heart breaking within her, Ellen comforted her weeping and distraught Henry with the words, "God will provide." And somehow He did.

When a cow became infected, the entire batch of milk would be tainted and would have to be dumped.

"God will provide." And somehow He did.

Henry and Ellen had no insurance. Earlier they had taken out an insurance policy, but when they entered a claim, it was denied because of something in fine print that had not been explained properly to them. All the hard earned money they had paid in to the company was lost. They were so devastated they never took out an insurance policy again. They resolved to put their trust in God instead of a flawed human organization.

When family members suffered broken limbs, surgeries, dental bills and hospital bills, there was no insurance.

"God will provide." And somehow He did.

When Ellen became pregnant with Randy, in the summer of 1946, serious health issues developed. The doctor warned that her life would be in danger if she delivered this baby. What a terrible predicament for Ellen and Henry! How they must have worried and prayed for God's guidance. The idea of terminating a human life went against everything they believed in; yet, to place Ellen's life in danger was unthinkable. How would Henry manage to take care of six children and a newborn without his beloved Ellen?

Randall Henry was born a healthy baby in March of 1947. Ellen came through the delivery; however, after the complications and trauma of that pregnancy, Ellen required a hysterectomy. She and Henry would have no more children. Ellen always thought of Randall as her miracle baby.

"God will provide." And somehow He did.

When Henry worked for Andrew, he was in a subordinate position, subject to decisions made by Andrew and while he didn't have the risks, neither did he enjoy the full profits. Then when he did own the farm outright, he reaped all the profits, but he was vulnerable to the risks - a "Catch 22."

"God will provide." And somehow He did.

Ellen kept the hardships and money problems from her children as best she could. They may have sensed that there were problems and they certainly knew they weren't enjoying many frills, but they were comfortable and learned to enjoy nature and the simple pleasures of life. They had food, clothing, a home and most important, they had parents who loved them and loved and supported each other and taught them the truths of the bible - taught them to fear God.

Ellen put up a strong front and many times when her heart must have been breaking with fear and worry, she never let on to her children that anything was wrong. She bolstered Henry's spirits as well. She had said, "God will provide," so many times, even she came to believe it.

It was as though there was a bank somewhere where

money could be gotten if needed. Indeed Ellen was like a bank herself.

"Mother - that was the bank where we deposited all our hurts and worries." [9]

"Give and it shall be given unto you; good measure, pressed down and shaken together and running over, shall men give into your bosoms. For with the same measure that ye mete withal, it shall be measured to you again." Luke 6:38

Through all the ups and downs of farm life, Henry and Ellen had a tithing jar which sat in a prominent position on a shelf of the hutch in the dining room. Into this jar they faithfully placed ten percent of their earnings in good times and in bad. No matter if the cherry crop was poor or the milk was tainted -- ten percent of the earnings went into the jar first. They never wavered in their obedience to the Biblical command to set aside a portion for the Lord. This jar was a symbol of their belief that what they had was not really theirs but belonged to God. Even though they couldn't afford it, their tithing became a means by which they could reach out to help others and thus demonstrate God's love for them.

Ellen gave her faith flesh and bones by adopting a Chinese orphan through World Vision, Inc. This child became a family project and everyone participated in packing yearly Christmas gift boxes and regular care packages of money and clothing throughout the year. Henry and Ellen's belief in God's promises became so strong, they couldn't afford *not* to tithe and reach out to others in need.

"God will provide." And somehow He did --over and over and over again. Each time they stretched their faith muscle, it became stronger for the next time.

"Blessed is the man that trusteth in the Lord, and whose hope the Lord is. For he shall be as a tree planted by the waters that spreadeth out her roots by the river, and shall not see when heat cometh, but her leaf shall be green; and shall not be careful in the year of drought, neither shall cease from bearing fruit." Jeremiah 17:7,8

"This book of the law shall not depart out of thy mouth; but thou shalt meditate therein day and night, that thou mayest observe to do according to all that is written therein: for then thou shalt make they way prosperous, and then thou shalt have good success." Joshua 1:8

In 1957, Henry purchased the farm from Andrew. Though Andrew still puttered around the farm and was available for advice, for the first time, Henry was in charge. Now the profits were entirely his but so were the risks.

As the years went by the children wended their way from childhood through adolescence, puberty and young adulthood; their life experiences played out within the family, the school and the church.

Henry, the devout father, toiled to provide for the needs of his family and set for them a daily routine of prayer and bible reading, while, through it all, like a thread running through the fabric of their lives, was the influence of Ellen, a God-fearing mother who loved her children and instilled in them qualities of hard work, diligence and faith and trust in God. In addition she encouraged them to be independent and to pursue their dreams and ambitions.

Each one brought special joys and special challenges. As rewarding as it was to watch them mature, it must have been disconcerting at times for Ellen to see her own traits of independence and perspicaciousness reflected back to her in her children, now young adults themselves.

The church played such a prominent role in their lives that with decisions regarding their children, Ellen and Henry always had to consider what the church dictated and whether their children's actions presented a stumbling block to others.

In addition Henry served on the consistory, the church's governing body, so it behooved him to uphold their rules. This was a source of friction as the children matured and began to question many of these rules and regulations. Over time, with the increasing influences of personal reading, Maranatha and Winona Lake, Henry's faith matured and he came to place people before creeds and love before church policy.

Marilyn, being the oldest, was a trailblazer, on issues such as dating, going to movies, dancing and using cosmetics for the first time. When she went off to college, Ellen and Henry must have been proud even though they hated to see their first child leave the nest. Roger kept his parents on their toes by playing the devil's advocate and challenging their religious beliefs. Judi, too, loved a good argument. Health issues in high school forced her to switch high schools, from Muskegon to one, closer by, in Shelby. Wendell, who had always dreamed of buying the farm from his dad, negotiated the purchase of the farm and Andrew's house. Joan's caregiver tendencies blossomed early and Ellen and Henry encouraged her to enter nursing school. They encouraged Janet's musical talent by finding her a more advanced music teacher. Her shy and reclusive behaviors, which began in elementary school and continued into high school, were a source of concern for them. Randy, the youngest, had the house to himself his last three years in high school.

There was plenty of joy, worry and challenge to go

around. And then, before they knew it, the nest was empty and everyone had gone -- everyone except Wendell, who returned from his tour of service with the Military Police in Albuquerque, New Mexico, to work alongside his father on the farm.

Wendell had always dreamed of becoming a dairy farmer. He had enrolled in the dairy program at Michigan State University before leaving for the service. In 1968 he married and finalized the purchase of the farm. Andrew and Jane built a house in New Era, so Wendell and his new bride, Ruth, moved into their house, the original homestead.

And, so Henry sold the farm he had lived on his entire life but had owned outright for just eleven years.

Selling the farm to Wendell and knowing that the family tradition would be carried on for another generation must have been a very happy and fulfilling occasion for Henry and Ellen.

With all their children gone and the farm sold, they had time to slow down, relax and enjoy life. The sale of the farm, along with the inheritance money they received from their parents, relieved them of the money problems they had dealt with for so many years. Now they could afford to travel. They toured the continental US, Hawaii and Europe, though Henry always claimed his favorite spot was right at home on the farm, sitting in his recliner or out on the porch.

They had time to read and putter in the garden and the flowerbeds. Ellen kept her rose beds and flower gardens, but cut down on the size of the vegetable garden since there were only two mouths to feed now instead of nine.

She pursued her knitting, crocheting, tatting, embroidery and took up quilting. She handcrafted over 75 quilts by herself, only needing Henry's help with the final assembly of the quilt squares.

They fixed up the house and renovated the basement, putting in a pool table, where they spent many happy hours, shooting pool. The scary ringer washing machine had long since been replaced with a modern washer and dryer. Canning and freezing were now options instead of necessities.

They ate out whenever they wished. They took leisurely rides in the country and enjoyed their children and grandchildren.

All the while, under Wendell's ownership, the farm was being transformed from a small 80-acre farm into a large dairy enterprise. Gone were the orchards, the asparagus patches, the bean fields and the potatoes. The fields were green with alfalfa and corn for silage. Huge barns and pastures sprang up. Large self-propelled machinery replaced the horses and the old style tractors.

Henry and Ellen watched the transformation with amazement and pride. Henry could help out on the farm as much or as little as he wished. Small, but important, jobs like feeding the calves helped him to feel a part of things.

And so they grew older with each other and with their Lord.

When they passed the torch on to a new generation, they left the days of eking out a living, pinching pennies, crop failures and daily struggles behind them; however, there were new challenges looming on the horizon.

Henry and Ellen would continue to experience joys and sorrows with all of their children; yet, there is no loss as painful as the death and estrangement of one's children. Henry and Ellen would experience both with their children Judith and Randall.

♥

CHAPTER TWO

Accepting The Unacceptable

"And the king was much moved, and went up to the chamber over the gate, and wept: and as he went, thus he said, 'O my son Absalom, my son, my son Absalom! Would God I had died for thee, O Absalom, my son, my son!'" II Samuel 18:33 (NIV)

My sister, Judi, died on July 5, 1987. She was 48 years old and in the prime of her life. Everyone in our family was in shock, but the news hit my mother especially hard. She was stunned beyond belief. As she struggled to comprehend the unthinkable and accept the unacceptable, her spirit sagged and slowly ebbed away. She appeared dazed and lifeless. Finally, paralyzed by grief and despair, she withdrew to her room. My father guarded her privacy and along with her husband, my siblings and me, saw to the details of the funeral, answered the phone and greeted friends and relatives who stopped by with their condolences.

My parents' home was hushed and quiet, almost eerie. While we grieved one family member, we worried about another. I remember passing by my mother's bedroom once when my father was leaving. My mother lay facing the windows, the bedcovers, like a shroud, covering her. So still, so quiet, so lifeless. I was scared. I was heartbroken over my sister's death. Now I was worried and anxious about my mother. It seemed that we were losing her too.

Parents never expect their children to die before they do. It's not normal - not the natural order of things. For a mother to lose a child carried in her womb and nursed at her breast, the pain must be excruciating - a wound, deep and gaping. Adding to the pain, was the fact that Judi's death was not a clean wound but one tainted with hurt and bruised with pain.

Judi was the third child in the family. She seemed to have a normal childhood, but problems surfaced during her high school years. She started high school in Muskegon, Michigan, but severe headaches, perhaps caused by the long commute - about an hour each way, forced her to transfer to a high school closer by, in Shelby, Michigan.

The headaches resurfaced in college along with new aggravations of skin problems and thinning hair. Once she used a heating lamp on her skin and burned herself badly. She started spending abnormal amounts of time in bed.

My parents didn't know what to do or how to help. Some insidious evil was wreaking havoc on their household. They couldn't understand how a daughter so bright, athletic, competitive and talented could be incapacitated with hopelessness and despair. Not much was known about depression back then and it certainly wasn't accepted as a disease.

Judi loved sports and the out-of-doors. She played volleyball, tennis and softball and loved canoeing, kayaking, hiking and horseback riding. She rode Roger and Wendell's spirited horse, Prince, bareback. She was intensely competitive but often her desire - her need to win, interfered with her enjoyment of sports, games and life. It seemed that she needed to prove herself – but to whom? Games that started out as fun often turned into fiercely tense situations. Friendly discussions degenerated into battles of wits and unpleasant argumentative debates. She was constantly questioning ideas and beliefs. She seemed driven in everything she did. She had no peace.

Judi did not imbibe the faith that came naturally to her parents. While they took the bible at face value, she was the devil's advocate, constantly questioning their beliefs. They attempted to reason with her and persuade her but alas, the old saying is true: "A {woman} convinced against {her} will is of the same opinion still."

Her attitude saddened my parents deeply. While Judi attempted to trim God down to a size and mentality she could understand, my parents worshipped a covenant God, awesome, personal, gracious and just.

She married the summer after college graduation and moved to California, where she and her husband, Wayne, taught for a number of years. While in California, their first son, Brent, was born. They returned home at the end of that teaching year to be closer to their families. Their second child, Erik, was born while they were home and then, after a few years, they moved to Wyoming, where Wayne had a teaching position. After a year, they returned home -- this time for good.

They bought a small, centennial farm outside of Whitehall, Michigan and settled down. With both boys in school, Judi enrolled in a doctoral program at Michigan State University. She was bright and excelled in her studies. She received her degree and got a teaching job at a local college.

Though Judi and her family had many good times, the depression was always there, lurking in the shadows, like a snake, waiting to strike. Her down times seemed to get progressively worse - longer, deeper and blacker than before.

In her despair Judi often turned to her mother for help and comfort. My mother was always there for her and many times remarked that she would gladly have borne the pain in her stead. She would have given her life for Judi's well being.

Judi had had shock treatments, had been hospitalized and had been under the care of a psychiatrist. She was diagnosed with a chemical imbalance but the prescribed medication did not seem to be effective and furthermore, it evened out her emotions so that she felt like a robot, incapable of feeling emotional highs or lows. She viewed taking pills as a sign of weakness and resisted taking the medication. Her worst fear, she relayed to my mother, was that she would be committed to an institution for the rest of her life.

In a tragic turn of events, Judi never had to face that fear. That dreaded snake emerged from the shadows, seized her in a death grip and engulfed her in blackness and despair. Like a python with its prey, it coiled itself around her, suffocated her and squeezed out of her, her aspirations, her dreams, her expectations for herself and her boys, her questions, her searchings, her yearnings. All of it gone, smothered, shattered.

In the throes of depression's deadly grip, she convinced

herself that her husband, children and family would be better off without her. She spent her last days in the intensive care unit of the hospital, hooked up to tubes with charcoal running relentlessly through her infected system. At one point she seemed to rally and was able to converse with members of the family, but in the end, her system could not withstand the shock it had suffered. Judi's life was snuffed out.

We were paralyzed with disbelief and grief. My mother did not visit her in the hospital. Knowing her, she was home on her knees praying. But what could she pray? When she was in the grip of depression, Judi's life was a hell on earth and one of the attending physicians in the hospital had told us that if she did recover in the hospital, she would be institutionalized, since she was a threat to herself and society. So, completely at the end of herself and lacking hope for her precious daughter, what did my mother pray?

Some have described this prayer as the most difficult to pray because it requires a complete relinquishing of one's desires and needs to God. One needs to be prepared to do His will before even knowing what it is. As a student of faith, Ellen was learning that you cannot ask for God's will to be done and then decide whether or not to accept the results. She was learning to trust that His way was best, but when she lost Judi, her faith was tested as never before.

And so she lay apart in her room, quiet and still.

"I Come to the Garden Alone..."

"Ellen."
Ellen, curled up in a fetal position, laid on her bed, spent

and still.

"Oh, my Lord, is it You," she whispered?

"Yes, Ellen."

Quietly, through her tears, "Oh, my Lord, you found me."

"Yes, my child. I am here."

"My Lord! I have lost my precious Judi." A wail, almost primeval, pierced the air.

"Yes, my dear one, I know."

Ellen's spoke through her sobs, her voice so soft it could hardly be heard. "Lord, 'Mine eye also is dim by reason of sorrow, and all my members are as a shadow.'"

"I know. I am here with you."

With a heart-rending wail, "Oh, my God, I loved her so. I prayed so hard that she would be healed. Why? Why? Why, my Lord, did she have to die?"

"It is not for us to know, my dear Ellen. But I know how much you loved her. I know that you would have borne her pain in her stead. You would have given your life for her."

"Oh, yes, my Lord, yes. She suffered so and I could not help her. I tried but it wasn't enough. It wasn't enough!"

Sobs racked her body. "Have mercy upon me O Lord, for I am in trouble: mine eye is consumed with grief, yea, my soul and my belly"

"I know. Do not try to talk, my child. Just rest. Rest in me. Let me bear your grief and suffering. Give it all to me."

Then fresh sobs. "Oh, my Lord, her boys. How will they cope without their mother? She loved them so. She tried so hard to be a good mother to them but, but it was just too much for her. She just couldn't go on any more."

"I know. But remember, I loved her too. I love her still. It is written: '...weeping may endure for a night, but joy cometh in the morning.'"

Gradually her sobbing ceased and Ellen lay still for a time.

Then, "Oh Lord, please be with her husband, Wayne and her boys, Brent and Erik. They need You. And, and if you will stay with me, I will try to go on."

"You have my Word, dearest Ellen. I will never leave you nor forsake you. You have loved deeply and well. It will be enough."

Ellen was exhausted from her struggle.

Finally, "I will try to get up now and go to my family, my Lord."

"That is good. They need you. Your love has made you whole. Go in peace."

(The Scripture passages in *In The Garden* are from Job 17:7, Psalm 31:9 and Psalm 30:5 - KJV)

In a haze of grief and gloom, the funeral arrangements were finalized. We prepared to say a final goodbye to our beloved Judi. We did not expect my mother to attend the visitation or the funeral.

Then, suddenly, there she was. She emerged from her room. We were surprised and a bit startled, not knowing what to expect. A noticeable peace and serenity, almost other worldly, radiated from her being. She spoke and began doing a few everyday duties with a calm, seemingly detached manner. She attended the visitation that evening and the funeral the next day. Though quiet and subdued, she carried herself with grace and graciousness. Her manner helped us give Judi's life and struggle a measure of dignity and respect. We marveled.

Though she was never the same after Judi's death and carried her grief to her own grave, the peace and serenity she exhibited when she emerged from her room stayed with her the rest of her days.

Hardship was no stranger to my mother. She and my father had honed their faith on the farm, suffering through crop failures, unfair treatment, loneliness and isolation and a pregnancy and birth that threatened Ellen's life. Her youngest son, Randy, after serving in Viet Nam had broken off all communication with the family. Judi's problems had been a source of worry for years. Roger, in the military service, was often in harm's way. They worried when Wendell's negotiations for purchase of the farm broke down. Marilyn was teaching and living away from home and there were concerns with Joan's and Janet's welfare as well.

They brought all of life's hardships and adversities to their God in prayer and believed that whether or not their prayers were answered the way they would have wanted, His way was the best way. My mother, the stronger of the two, had nerves of steel. She never gave up.

But when Judi died, something in my mother broke. She came to the end of what she was capable of dealing with, even with the promises of the Bible and prayer. It was at that point that she withdrew to her room.

It was there Jesus found her. In her pain and loss she did not forsake her Savior and Lord but rather she clung to Him for help and solace.

In her time of total despair, emptiness, selflessness and yieldedness to God's will, her Lord found her, "in the garden." He touched her and made her whole.

Filled with His spirit, she became a new person in Christ - like gold tried in the fire.

That experience changed my mother's life forever. It was a defining moment; a moment for eternity. From that point, she lived with acceptance instead of mere resignation. And that distinction made all the difference in her life - the difference that enabled her, after a time, not just to survive in her faith, but to thrive.

CHAPTER THREE

The Pain Of Estrangement

"And He spake this parable unto them saying, What {mother} of you, having an hundred sheep, if {she} lose one of them, doth not leave the ninety and nine in the wilderness, and go after that which is lost, until {she} find it?" Luke 15: 3-4 (NIV)

One of the most painful things my mother had to deal with in her lifetime was being estranged from her youngest son, Randall. To her dying day she held out hope that she would see or hear from him one last time but it was not to be.

Randy was nineteen and in his first year of college when he left home to fight in the Viet Nam war. My mother could not have known then that their relationship would be altered forever.

My father was not a soldier. During World War II he received a deferment to stay home with Ellen and manage the family farm. All three of their sons, however, served in the military.

Roger, the oldest, finished his second year of college and enrolled in the Pilot Training program at Pensacola, Florida. When the Viet Nam war broke out, he was deployed to the Far East for four months on an aircraft carrier. He served as a member of the Military Assistance and Advisory Group. Wendell served in the Military Police Corps in Albuquerque, New Mexico. His time was up just as the Viet Nam war broke out. Randy enlisted in the army and was sent to Viet Nam with the 24th regiment.

As proud as they were to have their sons serve their country, they must have hated to see them leave.

Though Roger and Randy were in Nam at the same time, they never saw each other. Roger conducted bombing missions, while Randy fought the enemy up close and personal in the jungles.

In the beginning, he rode shotgun on convoys, an extremely dangerous position. Later he joined the Long Range Reconnaissance program. He worked in small groups, in cooperation with Special Forces units to capture North Vietnamese soldiers and turn them over to Army interrogators or to the CIA. His groups would set enemy ambushes and capture the stragglers.

He experienced horrors beyond imagination, difficult for any soldier to deal with, let alone a young man just nineteen years old. On one occasion his group was marching Viet Cong prisoners to the Army base for interrogation. They passed through a South Vietnamese village and were intercepted by a war leader, who persuaded them to turn the prisoners over to him for safekeeping. This they did, but to their horror, he marched the prisoners up a hill, called out his soldiers, and used the prisoners for target practice, while Randy and his fellow soldiers looked on helplessly.

When the war was over, all three returned home. Roger married and eventually moved to Virginia, where he took a position with the Department of Defense in Washington DC. Wendell returned home to work with Henry and eventually bought the family farm, married and settled into Andrew's house, the original homestead. While they seemed to reenter civilization with some measure of normalcy, things seemed different for Randy from the start.

I remember the day he returned from overseas. My husband and I picked him up from a military warehouse in Chicago. What do you say to someone who, the day before, has been fighting in the jungles and corralling enemy troops? He must have been an emotional wreck, yet there we were, riding down the highway, discussing the weather and attempting small talk.

Randy came home to work on the farm. He moved into the old chicken coop next door to my parents. It was renovated into one large room that became his bedroom, library, and workplace. He amassed a serious collection of books and records and spent his spare time reading and writing. He ate his meals with my parents and would often stay afterwards to discuss a book, play chess with my mother and a game of pool downstairs with my father. Except for the time he spent with his parents and his work contacts, Randy was pretty much a loner.

He seemed content living and working on the farm. He didn't discuss his time in Viet Nam, but from the information he shared with Roger and Wendell, we knew it had been traumatic. My parents were happy to have him home and cherished the time he spent with them. They must have worried about him and wondered how long his time at home would last.

Perhaps my mother remembered a summer Sunday

evening, some years earlier, when she called up to say goodnight to Randy only to find that he wasn't there. An open window and a "sheet rope" tied to the bedpost signaled he was gone. Wendell and I were the only children home at the time and I remember the evening well. Wendell and my father set out in the car to find Randy. My mother led me into her bedroom, where she knelt by her bed, recited psalms, and prayed. Her prayers were answered and later that evening Randy was found but worries must have remained. Why had Randy run away? Would he leave again?

Now, he was home but it didn't last long. After about five years Randy left the farm and reenlisted in the army. He was sent to Europe on a peacetime mission. My parents were sad to see him leave. My mother phoned him weekly. From her conversations with him and his commanding officer, she believed he was doing well. I received a postcard from him displaying the Dresden Opera House, where he had enjoyed a Mozart opera. His message was cheerful and upbeat.

Then one evening my mother's world came crashing down. She had made her weekly phone call to Randy. After a lengthy wait, his commanding officer came to the phone. He informed my mother that Randy would not talk to her. Though she asked for an explanation, he had no answers. Randy had requested that she not call again.

My mother was stunned, hurt and confused. Sometime later my parents received word that Randy was being discharged from the service and returning to the U.S. My parents were not given any information about his whereabouts, the reason for his discharge or his condition. To complicate matters further, it became known that he had been communicating with Senator Guy VanderJagt, the

U.S. Congressman from Michigan. Did this have something to do with his refusal to talk, his silence and discharge? It was mystifying, troublesome and deeply painful for my parents.

After a time Randy was located in the state of Washington. My mother believed that if Randy could be found he would return home. She implored Wendell to visit. How she must have prayed while he was away! When he returned home, however, the news was not good. Randy had been aloof, cool and distant. He treated Wendell like a stranger, showing no emotion when Wendell relayed to him my parents' love and desire to see him. He seemed relieved when Wendell left.

My mother's hopes were shattered.

She continued to send Randy weekly letters, tins of homemade cookies and yearly Christmas packages. When her gifts were not returned, she assured herself that he had received them. She continued to pray that God might change and soften Randy's heart.

Years went by. My mother, not content to give up on her dream of being reunited with Randy, asked Roger to visit. Since they had both served in Viet Nam, she hoped Randy might relate to him. Roger received the same reception: coldness, disinterest and obvious annoyance.

Now my mother had to come to grips with the grim reality that Randy did not want to have anything to do with his family.

How does a mother accept the unacceptable? How does she accept the truth that a son, carried in her womb and nursed at her breast, nurtured in love and raised in a Christian home, rejects her? How many bottles would it take to hold the tears she must have shed in her pain and sorrow? I've often wondered if it would have been easier for her if Randy had died in the jungles of Viet Nam.

In her grief and despair, she threw herself on the mercies of her Lord. Up until now her focus had been on her need to be reunited with her beloved son; however, once she realized she was helpless to make that happen and her prayers might not be answered as she hoped, she came to the end of herself - her ego, her hopes, her needs and her desires.

In the garden...
Ellen was in the garden, weeping as she bent low to pull up the carrots. She snipped off the tops and dropped the sooty orange taproots into her basket.
"Ellen."
"Oh, my Lord, you have come."
"Yes, my dear Ellen. I am here."
"Oh, my Lord, alas, my son, my son, Randy..."
"I know..."
"You know that both Roger and Wendell went out to see him and..."
"Yes, Ellen, I know."
"Then you know that he is not coming home?"
She sank to her knees in the carrot tops and sobbed uncontrollably.
"'Have mercy upon me, Oh Lord, for I am in trouble: mine eye is consumed with grief, yea, my soul and my belly." My son, Randy, my youngest son, the one I was not supposed to have, the one Henry and I prayed for daily, the one whose birth was a miracle...my Randy...'"
Her voice trailed off in a wail of grief.
"Yes, Ellen, I know."
"Oh, my Lord, oh my Lord..." she could not go on.
It was quiet for a time in the garden, the silence broken

occasionally by sounds of weeping and sobbing.

Then, "'Ellen. It is written: '...this is my beloved Son, in whom I am well pleased.'"

Ellen paused, her body shuddering with the onslaught of her sorrow. His words, so familiar, yet so shocking in their familiarity. She shook her head in bewilderment.

"What, what, my Lord, what are you telling me?"

For a moment, she set aside her pain in an attempt to discern the meaning of His words. A sudden revelation broke through her pain like a lightning flash.

She spoke softly, her voice full of wonderment.

"Oh, my Lord. Yes, of course. I, I understand I think. A beloved Son, yes, a beloved Son.... Your father in heaven gave you up, my Lord, to die on the cross for the sins of the world - for Henry, for our children, for me - for Randy!"

The answer came back sad and strained.

"Yes, my dearest Ellen. As it is written: 'Surely He hath borne our griefs and carried our sorrows: yet we did esteem his stricken, smitten of God and afflicted. But he was wounded for our transgressions, he was bruised for our iniquities; the chastisement of our peace was upon him; and with his stripes we are healed.'"

"Oh, oh, my Lord, then You know how I feel!" Ellen exclaimed, "Oh, I loved Randy so! I love him still! I miss him so! I cannot go on without him! Please help me!"

There was panic in her voice.

"I know how much you hurt, my dearest. I know it hurts to love someone."

"Yes, oh yes, my Lord. I love him with all my heart, with all my strength and with all my mind."

She paused, nonplussed, afraid she had spoken amiss.

But the voice smiled through her pain.

"Ellen...Ellen...you have a great capacity to love. That is good. And, remember, I love Randy too."

"Yes, my Lord, but to love is to be vulnerable. It is because I love Randy so that my heart is breaking."

The voice was firm like a teacher's - the voice of a master. "Ellen. Love is the way, the only way, if you desire to follow Me. Hear these words, my child: '...but to this {one} will I look, even to him that is poor and of a contrite spirit and trembleth at my word.'"

Ellen, quietly, "Oh, my Lord, the things You say are too much for me. I do want to follow You and walk in Your ways but I need help. Will You help me, my Lord?"

"The way of love and acceptance is difficult my child."

"Yes, my Lord, but You have promised to walk with me, yes?"

"Yes, my dearest. I will never leave you nor forsake you. Now, finish your chores and go to your family. Go in peace and remember these words: '...for he hath said, I will never leave thee nor forsake thee.'"

Then He was gone.

Ellen continued down the row, pulling up the rest of the carrots, pondering everything her Lord had told her. A quiver of hope shot through her soul and steadied her in her despair.

When her basket was full, she straightened and walked slowly toward the house where her family was waiting. (Scripture verses in *In The Garden* are from Psalm 31:9, Matthew 3:17, Isaiah 53:4-5, Isaiah 66:2 and Hebrews 13:5)

Thus did God fill His humble and obedient servant, Ellen, with a new spirit of strength and hope.

Now she was able to place Randy's good above the needs

and desires of herself. She had always known that Randy's experiences in Viet Nam were traumatic. She understood that it was difficult for him to return to life as normal. Though she didn't understand why he felt it necessary to alienate himself from the family, she came to respect his decision.

She was thankful that Randy had a job, that his fellow workers thought well of him, that he seemed healthy, physically and emotionally, and that he was not a burden or detriment to society. And even though, after a time, she stopped sending the care packages, she never stopped praying for his well-being, for his soul, or for a miracle that would bring him home. She might not see Randy this side of heaven, but she prayed fervently that he would come to find the Lord and that she would see him in heaven one day. She never stopped loving him.

The indwelling of God's spirit had given her a divine perspective and enabled her to continue living with a peace and calm that defied all human understanding.

Some time later, my parents' pastor informed them that the church had decided to excommunicate Randy - a painful blow indeed. Their church, where they had been members and had faithfully served all their lives, was a small, strict conservative body of believers. In following their rules of governance, they was essentially banning Randy from the communion of the saints and pronouncing him a reprobate. Though my parents were staunch believers in the church as the (imperfect) body of saints on earth, their faith was always bigger than the institution.

Once God put His mark upon them and they were filled with His spirit, they were untouchable and unflappable. They accepted the church's decision; yet, in their hearts, they, never, for a moment, gave up hope that Randy would, one day, be saved.

Ellen was emotionally strong by nature and a survivor, yet, she could never have come to accept Randy's alienation by her own strength and willpower. Trying to "guts it out," on her own, would have led to bitterness, complaining and resignation, which was not my mother. She was never a passive believer. She accepted God's will wholeheartedly because she believed that God's way was the best way, for now and for eternity.

To such a faithful, yielded and accepting soul as my mother, God's reward is hope and joy. Not gushy, giddy or frivolous jollity, but a deep, lasting jubilance, which only God can impart.

Some years later when Judi died, we notified Randy through a contact at the college in Washington, where he was employed as a custodian. We heard nothing. We left him a message when my father died. Again, we heard nothing. Then, in the last days of my mother's life, we left him a message telling him that his mother was dying. After so many years of silence we wondered if he would be moved to respond. We were told that Randy would not talk to us. We never heard from him again.

I watched my mother grieve over Randy but it was not until I had sons of my own that I came to realize the pain she must have borne over his estrangement. As I think back, I envision her, sitting on the porch, watching and waiting for her long lost son to call, write, or come home. I am overcome with emotion. It is a story fraught with eternal significance, for though it does not have a happy ending, I believe the whole story has not yet been told. God will have the last word and I believe He works miracles in the lives of believers, like my mother.

"He that hath an ear, let him hear what the Spirit saith unto the churches; To {her} that overcometh will I give to eat of the hidden manna and will give {her} a white stone, and in the stone a new name written, which no man knoweth saving he that receiveth it." Revelation 2:17

I'm so bold as to think that the name written on that white stone could just be "Randy."

CHAPTER FOUR

Heaven Tugging, Always Tugging

"I am crucified with Christ; nevertheless I live; yet not I, but Christ liveth in me: and the life which I now live in the flesh I live by the faith of the Son of God, who loved me and gave himself for me." Galatians 2:20 (NIV)

Life went on for Henry and Ellen without their precious Judi and their beloved Randy. For some couples, hardships present so many challenges and pain that their relationship is strained, sometimes to the point of breaking; however, that was not the case with my parents. Family challenges, Judi's tragic death and Randy's estrangement only brought them closer together. After all, God was the bedrock of their marriage. Along with the burdens came the strength to bear them. Their faith continued to grow strong by stretching.

Now that they were getting older, traveling was more difficult. They still managed to visit their children, Roger and Joan, and their families, who lived out of state. And though Ellen was always ready to go places, she realized that Henry's health was failing and that travel was getting more difficult for him.

On the farm, though, there was always something happening and they were right in the middle of it.

They had learned how to be content with a simple life. Though they had been poor, their hearts were full with the promises of God, their family, friends and nature – things money cannot buy. They knew well that you can have all the money in the world, but if your heart is not full, you are poor.

Up to this time they had enjoyed relatively good health. Ellen had had a pacemaker installed. Henry had suffered an aneurysm, but the family had decided against surgery and the aneurysm seemed to be under control. He also suffered from diverticulosis, which made eating tenuous and uncomfortable, but not life threatening.

Gradually Henry's health deteriorated and his memory began to wane. He began to confuse his children's names and, sadly, he was aware that he was confused. He confided to Wendell that he had a premonition his time would be up soon and asked Wendell to promise that he would take care of Ellen, when he was gone.

Henry was worried he would be a burden to Ellen and the family and might have to leave his beloved home. Life in a nursing home would have been tragic for him, so closely was his life tied to the farm and the house on the hill.

Then one morning, God tapped Henry on the shoulder.

He awoke, had breakfast, read a bit and then returned to bed, complaining that he didn't feel well. Shortly afterwards he died. He was 83 years old.

Ellen was inconsolable. So closely were their lives

intertwined after 60 years of marriage, it was as though part of her had been ripped away, leaving a gaping chasm of emptiness and pain. She was overwhelmed with grief.

When Henry died, my mother lost more than a husband. She lost her lover of a lifetime, her best friend, her spiritual partner and her helpmeet.

If someone does something nice for you, they are special, but if just being with someone is special, that is a sign of a unique, exceptional relationship. So it was with my parents. They only needed each other to make their world special and complete.

They lived together so long they resembled each other. They were two parts of a whole - almost mirror images of each other. Their marriage of 60 years was a true symbol of the Biblical description of Christ's relationship to His church.

To love completely is to be completely vulnerable and she was.

"In the garden..."
"Ellen." The voice, ever so sweet and low.
"Oh, my Lord. My Henry, my beloved Henry...he is gone, my Lord, he is gone." Her voice was wracked with sobs.
"Yes, my dear Ellen. I know. Henry has gone to be with His Lord." The voice, sweet and low.
"Oh my Lord. I loved him so. I miss him so." Her voice was laced with pain and anguish.
"Ellen. It is written: 'The Lord is nigh unto them that are of a broken heart; and saveth such as be of contrite spirit.'"

For a moment the sobbing ceased. Then she cried anew.
"Oh, my Lord, I do not wish Henry back. I know it was his

time to die. I know that he is in heaven and at peace. But it is hard to go on without him, my Lord. If it be your will, could I go to be with him? Would that be possible?"

The voice, sweet and low, took on the slightest twinge of firmness. "My dear Ellen, that is not for us to determine. It is written: 'Peace I leave with you, my peace I give unto you: not as the world giveth, give I unto you. Let not your heart be troubled, neither let it be afraid.'"

At His words, Ellen was quiet. Then, in the midst of her sorrow, a quiet feeling spread over her, almost surreptitiously, like a coverlet spread upon a featherbed. Peace, like a river, flowed into her soul, its rivulets filling every inlet and cove of her being.

Gradually her sobbing ceased, her grief, assuaged.

"It is enough, my Lord," words spoken quietly, obediently.

"My dear child. It is written: '...weeping may endure for a night, but joy cometh in the morning.'"

"I wonder if I can ever be happy again," she mused aloud.

"One day, my child. One day it will all become plain. Now go to your family. They too are grieving their father and grandfather."

"Yes, my Lord. I will go to them."

Then He was gone.

Ellen paused in the garden for a few moments. She wiped the tears from her eyes and with a sorrowful serenity in her heart, she went in to join her children.

(Scripture passages in this section are from Psalm 34:18, John 14:27 and Psalm 30:5,6)

The family gathered to make plans for Henry's visitation, funeral and burial. Ellen helped make the necessary decisions. She carried herself with grace and dignity through the visitation and funeral, as Henry was remembered and his body buried in the family plot in the cemetery, next to Benjamin and Winnie and Benjamin's brother John and his entire family, who had died so tragically many years earlier.

Henry's service and burial were a testimony to the power of the resurrection. He was remembered as a simple, humble, hard-working and God-fearing man. He was meek, gentle and honest. He attended church and was religious, but his spirituality could not be contained within the four walls of any church. Henry worshipped God daily in nature as he worked outside on the farm under His Father's heavenly dome. He studied the stars with a telescope and knew the names of the constellations. He could predict the weather by looking at the sky and the cloud formations. He could identify birds by their calls and their coats. He loved to read a wide variety of works including biography, history and poetry. He could recite entire poems. "Snowbound," by John Greenleaf Whittier, was one of his favorites. He read the bible daily and prayed without ceasing. He could recite bible passages from memory. He loved attending Maranatha and Winona Lake Bible Conferences. He loved feeding the calves and spraying Ellen's roses. He loved sitting in his recliner in the evenings as he and Ellen read their books and on the porch, in season, watching the sun set over the western hills. He witnessed to his faith with his mellow, tenor voice in the duets he sang with Ellen. He was a good, loving father.

Vance Havner, one of Henry's favorite country preachers, could have been describing Henry, when he wrote these words about his own father:

"Like Noah, father, got his family into the ark. I used to think he was a bit too strict, but I can see the point now. He could have compromised a little here and hedged a little there and dropped to the level of the average. He could have decided that maybe he was overdoing it and hidden behind the verse, 'Be not righteous overmuch.' But he was out to build with gold, silver and precious stones and would not be inveigled into trafficking with wood, hay and stubble. His life will stand the fire test, for he built soundly and managed to get some solid materials into the lives of his children as well." [1]

Henry had loved Ellen with all his heart and had been a faithful, loving husband for sixty years.

He was remembered for all of this at his funeral, but especially for the God he loved and served all his days.

Bereft and bereaved, Ellen, once again came to accept God's will and embrace His way for her life. It was typical of her to look for the good in a situation. Over time, she gave thanks that Henry had passed on before her because she knew how difficult it would have been for him to get along by himself. She was thankful he had died without having to suffer or become a burden to others – something she knew was a worry to him. He had died at home on his beloved farm, where he had lived for 83 years; yet, the house on the hill was a mere tent compared with his heavenly abode, where he was finally "at home" with his Lord for eternity.

Henry was certainly with his beloved Jesus and Ellen believed that she would one day be reunited with him in heaven. How she longed for that day to come!

CHAPTER FIVE

Home At Last

"Oh Death, where is Thy sting? Oh grave, where is thy victory?"
I Corinthians 15:55 (NIV)

With heaven tugging at her heart, Ellen journeyed on alone, without her beloved Henry, trusting in God to lead her through yet another passageway of her life.

She had her children and her son and daughter-in-law, Wendell and Ruth, lived next door; yet, she was bereft and lonely. She had lived with Henry for over sixty years and had become vulnerable with her complete love for him and their life together. When he died, a part of her was wrenched away, leaving a gaping hole of grief and sadness.

Life without Henry had lost its luster. The breeze seemed stifling, the birds' colors weren't as brilliant. The cricket's chirping wasn't as cheerful and the frogs' croaking not as comforting. The sunsets were not as spectacular. And, try as she might, she could no longer see Lake Michigan from the porch on a clear day. Henry's chairs on the porch and in the living room screamed "VACANCY!"

Ellen talked with Henry every evening after saying her

bedtime prayers, so thin was the veil separating them.

After a time of grieving Ellen continued on with her activities. Her heart wasn't totally in them but she tried. She resumed playing the organ at church and attended Golden Hour during the week. She sang and gave her weekly devotional at the nursing home. She did her weekly mentoring with children at the local school. She drove to Holland on Sundays after church to have dinner with her older daughter, Marilyn and her family. She visited her son Roger in Virginia and spent time with her daughter Joan in Illinois.

She went on a Caribbean cruise with Marilyn and Janet. Her worries about traveling disappeared when she was whisked through airports in a wheelchair, first to board the plane and cruise ship and first to disembark. Ever gregarious and outgoing, she chatted with the attendants and shared stories of her beloved Henry. She was treated like royalty.

She kept in touch with her grandchildren and made a special effort to be available for Judi's sons, Brent and Erik. A few years after Judi's death, her husband, Wayne, had remarried. Ellen was deflated when she heard that Judi would be replaced with another mate. She assumed there would never be another partner for Wayne, the way it was with her and Henry. Then Wayne contacted bone cancer and after a brief, valiant struggle, he died. Once again, the boys experienced tragedy and death. My mother tried to be there for them as much as she could. She and Erik spent time together every week playing games, going out for dinner and occasionally they went to a movie.

Ellen didn't have many relatives or friends her age left. Her parents, her sister Marie and her brother Arnie were gone. Henry's parents and two sisters were gone. Only her older brother, Henry Postema, and his wife, Millie, (Henry's younger sister), were still living. It hit Ellen particularly hard when Millie took ill and died. Another soul gone to heaven, where her own precious Henry and Judi and her parents were – where she longed to be herself. She would get discouraged and wonder why God had not called her home, as He had the others.

One winter evening she went out for dinner with her grandson, Erik. Upon returning home, she was walking from the garage to the house when she lost her balance and fell into a snowbank.

It was there her Lord found her.

"In the Garden..."
Ellen laid in the snow exhausted and weeping.
"Ellen." That familiar voice, sweet and low.
"Oh, my Lord." Her voice shivered in the snow.
Lovingly, "Ellen. What are you doing out here in the cold?"
"Oh, my Lord, I cannot get up. 'I am weary with my groaning; all the night make I my bed to swim; I water my couch with my tears. Mine eye is consumed because of grief; it waxeth old because of all mine enemies.'"
Tenderly, "Ellen. Please get up. The night grows dark."
"My Lord." She was too weary to go on. "My Lord, please, please let me die here," she moaned in anguish.
Gently, but firmly, "Ellen, is this how you wish to die? Out here in the dark in a snowbank?"
After a moment, "Please, my Lord, just end my life so I don't have to decide. I am too weary to go on. And I miss my Henry so. " She wailed into the night.
"Ellen, Ellen. If you stay here you will surely freeze to death. Is this how you wish to end your life, my dear one?"

Quietly, in a whisper, her teeth chattering with cold, "I, I thought I did, my Lord... It's just that I'm so tired. My strength is gone. It would be so easy just to stay here..."

Gently, "I know, Ellen. But you have never taken the easy way out. Have you forgotten that the Father will never give His children more to carry than what they are able to bear? Listen Ellen, for it is written: 'Wait on the Lord: be of good courage, and He shall strengthen thine heart: wait, I say, on the Lord.'"

With a little burst of life. "Psalm 27 - oh my Lord, that is one of my favorite psalms. How did you know?"

He smiled upon her.

Ellen was shivering and shaking with cold.

"If you will help me, my Lord, I will try to go on. Forgive me for feeling sorry for myself."

Lovingly, tenderly, "No matter, my dear Ellen. Now try to get up, please try."

Slowly, with great effort, Ellen rolled off the bank. She struggled to her feet.

"My Lord, go with me, I pray, please go with me." She could hardly get the words out, her teeth were chattering so.

"Ellen. Remember my promise. 'I will never leave you or forsake you. You have my Word.'"

"Yes, my Lord." She was shivering uncontrollably now. "I will go." With renewed strength of body and soul, Ellen trudged up the path, in the darkness, toward the house.

(Scripture passages in the In The Garden section are from Psalm 6:6,7 and Psalm 27:14)

Shortly after that episode, the family decided that Ellen, now in her eighties, needed company in the house. A live-in companion was hired and moved into one of the upstairs bedrooms. She was hired do the housework and some cooking and cleaning, but her main job was providing company for Ellen.

Ellen's mood perked up considerably. She enjoyed the hustle and bustle of activity, even though it was not her own. Her spirits improved; however, health problems were starting to take a toll.

Ellen's hearing was virtually gone and hearing aids weren't helping. Her eyesight was waning. No longer could she read, play the piano or knit, crochet and quilt - the activities that once had brought her such comfort and fulfillment.

The hearing and vision problems prompted Ellen to give up driving and organ playing. Her church held a special music Sunday in her honor.

Then early one morning, Bethany, the caregiver, heard a noise downstairs. When she went to investigate, she found Ellen on the floor by her bedside. Ellen was taken to the hospital in an ambulance. Tests indicated she'd had a stroke. She spent weeks, hospitalized, undergoing therapy. Not well enough to return home, she spent time in a skilled nursing facility in Holland, Michigan. She made some progress, but just wasn't herself. She appeared disoriented and confused in her strange surroundings. She returned home, where the family arranged for twenty-four hour nursing care.

Happy to be home once again, Ellen slowly regained her speech and lucidity; however, the stroke had taken an obvious toll on her strength. She was forced to use a wheelchair to get around and became increasingly dependent. In-home nurses helped get her up, bathed her, fixed her breakfast and then, if it was nice weather, got her situated on the porch in a medical recliner.

It was at this point, that Marilyn, Joan, and I, her

daughters, took turns spending a day each week with her. This gave Ruth, next door, some much-needed relief, but it also gave us an opportunity to spend time with our mother, one on one.

Occasionally she would invite her brother, Henry, to lunch.

We'd pick him up (at ninety, he wasn't driving anymore either) and bring him to the house. Ellen, always the gracious hostess, would preside over the meal, engaging Henry in conversation. Two weary pilgrims remembering a shared past. Then Henry's health failed and he went to live in the nursing home. Shortly after Ellen visited him, he died. Ellen attended Henry's funeral. Heaven tugging, always tugging...

It couldn't have been easy for my mother to grow old, helpless, dependent, and incontinent.

All her life she had dealt with challenges and whenever she came to the end of her will and resolve, she turned to her Lord for strength and succor. He had never failed her in time of need.

"Until you have given up yourself to Him, you will not have a real self." [1]

Her fighting spirit was evident one day while playing a game of chess with Roger, who was visiting from Virginia. "I'm going to beat you today," she announced as they set out the game pieces. "We'll see about that," replied Roger, gearing up for some competition. The game began. After a few plays, Ellen made a move and proclaimed, "Checkmate!" Surprised by her sudden, irregular, move, Roger sputtered, "Mom, you can't do that." With a smug little grin, Ellen replied, "I just did." The game was over.

Ellen had won.

She was a survivor, yet her failing strength was taking an obvious toll on her will and resolve. One day, I was present when she was sitting in her wheelchair and announced that she had to use the bathroom. I readied the bedpan. "No," she said firmly. "I am going to get up and use the bathroom myself." With that, she pressed down on the handles of the wheelchair, trying to get herself in a standing position. Again and again she tried but to no avail. She couldn't move herself even an inch off the seat. After repeated tries she slumped down in defeat. "I just can't do it," she whispered.

"In the garden..."
"Ellen."
Weeping, "Oh, my Lord, I am so weak. I cannot get up. I have no strength left."
Tenderly, "I know, my dearest Ellen."
"My flesh and my heart faileth..."
"My dear. It is written: 'The glory of the young is their strength: and the beauty of old{women} is the gray {hair}'"
Ellen laughed in spite of herself, a bit bitterly.
"I do not feel very splendid my Lord. Look at me. I cannot even get up on my own strength."
"That is true. Your splendor is no longer in your physical strength or your outward health. Your beauty comes from within and that can never be taken away from you."
Ellen thought about this a long while.
Then with a new resolve, "It is as you say my Lord. Be with me to the end I pray."
"...for eternity, my dear one. This will be your last hurdle. '...for your Father knoweth what things ye have

need of before you ask Him.'"
"Yes, my Lord. 'My flesh and heart faileth; but God is the strength of my heart, and my portion forever.'"
(Scripture verses used in the In The Garden section are from Psalm 73:26, Proverbs 20:29 and Matthew 6:8b)

"Many of us find life hard and full of pain. We cannot avoid these things; but we should not allow the harsh experiences to deaden our sensibilities, or make us stoical or sour. The true problem of living is to keep our hearts sweet and gentle in the hardest conditions and experiences." [2]

In spite of her failing health, my mother mellowed beautifully in her last years of her life. Somehow, through all the hardships, sufferings and pain, she had kept her heart sweet and gentle.

She was a fine example of "gracious dependency," so aptly described in *The Power of Positive Aging,* by Donna Devall.

Ms. Devall defines dependency as a giving up of control, a difficult but necessary thing for us to deal with as we age. [3]

One of the most difficult things for my mother to relinquish as she grew older and dependent, was being able to drive, something she had always relished. During their latter years together, as Henry's health began to fail, she had taken over the driving responsibilities and prided herself on doing it well. When her own health began to deteriorate it was with some trepidation that we approached her about giving up the keys. It was not only her safety we were concerned with but the safety of others. As much as she hated to give up something that was so much a part of her life and pride, this was all it took for her to agree that she would give it up. The thought that she might injure someone was not acceptable to her.

She had learned to give up control many times in her life on the farm, when Henry got sick, when Judi died, when Randy left home and when Henry died. Now she was faced with giving up control of her health. She adapted to depending on others and managed to get the care she needed without being too demanding. She was always genuinely appreciative of their help. Her caregivers, nurses, friends and family members loved being around her. Even in her dependent state, she always managed to give back something to those helping her.

Just as she had cleaned her house and weeded her garden, she carefully tended her life. She knew that a house left untended would be full of cobwebs, dust and dirt and a garden left alone would be rife with weeds and thistles. In the same way she realized that an undisciplined life, without daily bible reading and prayer, would lead to spiritual laxness and disorder.

As she neared the end she did her final spring cleaning. She had never felt right about jilting Henry and brought it up one day with Marilyn, who helped reassure her that both Henry and God had forgiven her for what she had done.

In a conversation with Roger she came to the realization that her problems with sister-in-law Lena might have been as much her fault as Lena's.

Gone were the animosities between her and Henry's parents as well, for Wendell recalled that after Andrew and Jane moved to town, he and his wife, Ruth and Henry and Ellen would go to their home for coffee on Sundays after church.

There were other things she had done she should not

have done; things she had not done she should have. She was totally open to admitting her sins and shortcomings when new information was made available to her. She knew that good works did not count for her salvation, but she wanted peace in her soul when she met her Maker.

She didn't allow herself or others much slack. She stood by the bible and its principles, walked the straight and narrow path and expected others to do the same, but her experiences had softened her and taught her that life is not always black and white with simple answers. It has its gray parts too.

People were always dropping by to see her. Young and old alike loved to visit and often would share their problems with her. She had an incredible presence, almost magnetic. You could tell her anything. She listened and didn't judge or evaluate; yet her opinions were valued. She had grown wise with age and experience.

It has been said, "To have suffered much, is like knowing many languages: it gives the sufferer access to more people." That was my mother.

Her grandchildren loved spending time with her. She was recovering from her stroke, when Roger's youngest daughter, Andrea, came to visit. They were chatting at the dining table, when Ellen cautioned, "I've had a stroke you know." She wanted Andrea to know that she might not be her old self. Later that weekend I watched her on the porch with grandchildren, Andrea, Erik, and my son, George. They were laughing and thoroughly enjoying themselves with their grandmother. She was right in the thick of things, smiling beneficently on their merriment.

What was amazing about these encounters was that she was the reason for them getting together. They were laughing because of her and with her, not in spite of her, a ninety-year old grandmother.

The last years of Ellen's life weren't her best years, health wise, but time spent with her, during these last years, was rich and rewarding. Moments spent with her were moments lived in the present - moments of eternity - kairos moments.

As her body withered and faded, something remarkable was happening to Ellen. She grew weaker, yet her spirit seemed to wax stronger. She was helpless, utterly dependent, incontinent and vulnerable. Her skin was as thin as an onion's; yet, she glowed with an inner radiance that was almost otherworldly. It was as though the sunshine of God's face was shining through her, this emptied, tired, humbled pilgrim. Being with her was like being on holy ground. We marveled.

Finally, realizing that our mother was not going to get better and wanting her to spend her last days with dignity and without pain, we invited Hospice to come in. Her medications were discontinued and now daughter, Joan, and daughter-in-law Ruth, both nurses, could relinquish their mother's health care to the Hospice nurses and just be daughters. A hospital bed was brought in and situated in the living room, where Ellen could look out over the countryside she loved so dearly. She would never leave that bed again, this side of Heaven.

The amazing thing was that Ellen was dying, yet her spirit seemed so very alive, so eager and ready was she to reach the Promised Land.

In this weakened, dying state, Ellen gave her final gift. She showed her family and loved ones how to die. As we sat with her, she would drift in and out of consciousness. Many times, she would awaken from her dozing and be talking, lucidly, with Henry, who was obviously nearby for her. We realized then, with some amazement, that Ellen was traveling back and forth on the pathway between earth and heaven. Sometimes it would take her a few moments to reenter this world. She'd appear a bit dazed and shaken as she rearranged herself and made the transition back to "reality." She seemed to be experiencing what many others, who have visited the "other side," have described, when they realize they must return to their bodies - they do so reluctantly because the experience of love and peace has engulfed them. [4]

Dying seemed to be a totally fearless and peaceful experience for Ellen. To be in the presence of eternity through our beloved mother, was a sobering, amazing phenomenon - an experience etched in memory, deeply powerful and life changing. In her last days, Ellen provided a primer in dying. It was her final gift.

Ellen had given many gifts throughout her lifetime. Even when she and Henry were poor, they always gave birthday and Christmas gifts, oftentimes handmade. Ellen's gifts were fashioned with love and care: quilts, knitted afghans, sweaters and scarves, crocheted doilies and snowflakes, and tablecloths fashioned with needlepoint and candlewicking. She always brought back gifts from her travels. She gave gifts for high school and college graduations and shower and wedding gifts. When the grandchildren were born, she handcrafted beautiful blankets. She gave gifts from her gardens and flowerbeds. One never left the farm without bouquets of peonies or snapdragons, ears of yellow sweet corn, red ripe tomatoes and luscious green Kentucky Wonder beans.

Most importantly, she and Henry gave the gift of themselves -- parents who loved and respected each other and lived together in harmony. They raised their children in a Christian home where prayer and scripture reading were part of the rhythm of the day. Ellen, especially, nurtured her children's gifts and talents and encouraged them to go to college. She encouraged them to be independent and to pursue their dreams. Most importantly of all, she was a God-fearing mother, who was an influence for good in the lives entrusted to her.

Now, at the end of her life, helpless and dying, she gave her family the quintessential gift. She showed us how to die. Isn't death the final enemy? Isn't facing one's death the ultimate test of life, the underlying cause of fear, anxiety and even psychosis? Ellen, by her example, erased that fear for her children and loved ones. She had lived trusting in her Jesus and now at the end, Jesus was bringing her home.

"In the garden..."

Ellen laid on her hospital bed. She seemed to be asleep. Suddenly, her eyes flickered. She gazed out over the hills. They seemed so very far away. She felt tired, so very tired.

"Ellen."

The voice was familiar, soft and oh so tender.

"My Lord, is it You calling?"

"Yes, Ellen. It is time."

"Time?" She seemed confused and puzzled. "Time, my Lord? Is it time for me to get up then? I think I have overslept. Oh, my Lord, it is late? I have work to do - beans to pick and snip, roses to tend, socks to darn." She rushed on...

"No, Ellen," with a smile, "no, my dearest. You have no chores to do today. "You have fought the good fight. You have run the race...your earthly chores are done."

Hesitantly, "My Lord, I do not understand."

"My dear Ellen. It is time to go. Today, your name will be called, by the One who formed you in the beginning of time."

Then, as His words broke through to her, yet hardly daring to believe their meaning, she exclaimed, "My Lord, my Lord, can it be true? Oh, I have waited so long for this moment!"

"Ellen, today you will enter into the joy of your Lord. Come, the angels are waiting to bring you home. Can you hear them singing?"

Ellen's voice was animated now. "Angels, my Lord? Yes, I can hear them. Yes, I see them in the distance. They are coming closer. And, someone is with them." Joy gushing forth like a geyser from the ground. "Who is that with them, my Lord? Can it be, yes it is - my Henry! Oh, my Lord, my Henry!" I am ready. I am ready to go home!"

"Earth recedes, Heaven opens before me. If this is death, it is sweet! There is no valley here. God is calling me and I must go!" [5]

On the morning my mother died, I stood, with my brothers and sisters, as the funeral home attendants placed a sheet over her dead body. The house had been filled with the sounds and activity of family members, Hospice nurses and volunteers and my mother's musings and reveries. Now it was eerily still and so, so deafeningly quiet. With my mother gone, the life had gone out of the house on the hill. I knew that she had "flown away" to her heavenly home where she was free of pain and sorrow, but as her body was wheeled away, I heard a voice from somewhere deep inside me cry out, "No! No! Don't take her away!" I didn't want her to go. It seemed so final. Even then I had no idea of the thunderous waves of loss and bereavement that would roll over me in the months and years to come.

After that day, it was difficult for me to be in the house. We did the necessary sorting and cleaning out of our mother's things and took items that that had special meaning and significance to us or our children. What was left over we gave away. After everything was cleared out, I returned to the house one other time but soon realized that being there without my mother present was strange and eerily unpleasant for me. Even Max, my dog, who had always accompanied me on my weekly visits, knew something was wrong that day. He nosed about every room in the house in search of her. Finally, he went and laid in a corner by himself. Without its homemaker, the house on the hill had lost its ambience, its spirit and soul.

Now when I visit the farm with my grandchildren, I walk up the hill before I leave for a look at the house. I have no desire to go in. I can only stand and stare at the windows. That is enough for me.

"There are certain people, who if they are absent, life seems harder to bear. Who are these people? These are the people who once sat close to you in Paradise." [6]

It was selfish of me I knew, but I wanted my days with her to go on forever, so special had she become. In her later years, she had become so very dear to me. But I knew she was where she had longed to be – with Henry, Judi, her parents and loved ones. She was probably playing the heavenly organ already, singing in the celestial choir, tending the ever-blooming roses and fashioning bouquets that would never wither or fade. How could I wish her back?

At her funeral, she was remembered as a wife, mother, grandmother, great grandmother, musician, reading mentor, nursing home volunteer, church member and friend. She was remembered for her quilts, her afghans, her home-cooked meals, her pies, and her crocheted snowflakes. There were cherished memories of visits to the home on the hill, lively games of Chess, Scrabble and Rook, animated discussions around the dining room table and quiet musings on the front porch. She was remembered for the God she loved and served. We sang her favorite hymns.

"My Jesus, I love Thee, I know Thou art mine,
For Thee all the follies of sin I resign.
My gracious Redeemer, my Savior art Thou,
If ever I loved Thee, my Jesus 'tis now.
In mansions of glory and endless delight.
I'll ever adore Thee in heaven so bright.
I'll sing with the glittering crown on my brow,
If ever I loved Thee, my Jesus, 'tis now." [7]

Ellen had often remarked she didn't need a mansion in heaven - a simple cottage would be enough for her and Henry. She had now realized what we have since learned: the word "mansion" does not refer to a place of opulence, but from the Greek, simply, "an abode, a resting place," -- much more to her simple tastes.

Her body was carried from the church to the majestic strains of Handel's, *The Hallelujah Chorus.* In the cemetery, her remains were gently laid to rest next to her beloved Henry in the family plot with her parents, Benjamin and Winnie and her Uncle John and his family.

After the interment, we stood staring at the gaping hole in the earth, which would hold the remains of our precious mother, grandmother, and great grandmother. Suddenly, a child's cry pierced the air. One of Ellen's great granddaughters, in a sudden realization of the finality of death, voiced our collective feelings. *NO! We didn't want her to die.*

Our mother was gone from us and the house on the hill forever. She had gone home. We were left to mourn her absence in our lives.

CHAPTER SIX

Final Gifts

"All along the Christian course, there must be set up altars to God on which you sacrifice yourself, or you will never advance a step."[1]

After my mother's death, a friend sent me the following poems:

> Daughters Who Lose Their Mothers
>
> Daughters who lose their mothers early
> Take their mother's place.
> For them it is maturity
> It is young grace.
>
> But this is different.
> Daughters who lose an elderly mother;
> They have no one left, between them and age.
> To keep old age away…
> No one to stand there and, smiling, defend
> Their sight from the end.

Mother, your eyes had always a smile,
Looking at me, thinking me always a child.
No one else could see how unaccountably young
And wild that child could be.
No one else knew.
I take your place now,
And that child has gone with you.

By Margery Mansfield [2]

With my mother's death all settled happiness,
All that was tranquil and reliable disappeared from my life.
There was to be much fun, many pleasures, many stabs of joy,
but no more of the old security.
It was sea and island now;
The great continent had sunk like Atlantis.

...C.S. Lewis [3]

The poems describe why losing your mother is such a significant and sobering event. I had not thought about the fact that, while your mother is alive, she stands between you and death, but when she dies, that buffer is gone and now you become the one standing in front of death for your children, as your mother did for you – an extremely sobering fact. Death seems more real and imminent. You feel suddenly vulnerable.

This dawning awareness, that I was the one standing between my children and death, was coupled with a renewed sense of appreciation for my mother and an interest in learning more about her life. I had witnessed her death. Now I wanted to walk in her shoes, to find out the secret of the peace and victory so evident at the end of her life.

Six years have passed since my mother left us and went to heaven - not ten years, but it's ample time for reflection. Her story is powerful and gripping. It is one of faith, trust, suffering, acceptance, joy, and love. Her earthly pilgrimage was a love affair with God from the very beginning.

Sebastian Barry, in his book, *The Secret Scripture*, writes, "But we are in mourning for our mothers before even we are born." [4]

If I had read this statement before my mother died, I might have passed over it, but now, reflecting on her death and life, it gives me pause. What can this mean? I think it must have something to do with God back when the world was without form and void.

"In the beginning, God created the heaven and the earth. And the earth was without form, and void; and darkness was upon the face of the deep. And the Spirit of God moved upon the face of the waters." (Genesis 1:1,2)

I've been taught that before God created the world -- even before He formed us, He was Love. Then, in His infinite love, the teaching goes, He brought the world into being and fashioned creatures to inhabit the world, but longing to have the deepest and closest relationship possible, He made the likes of us, placing a spark of divinity within our hearts, until, as St. Augustine said, "We are restless until we rest in Him."

"If I find in myself a desire which no experience in this world can satisfy, the most probable explanation is that I was made for another world." [5]

It is not difficult for me to personalize the theory, to believe that this loving God fashioned one named Ellen. He forms her in the womb, walks with her, molds her, shares in her suffering, protects her, guides her, sets His mark upon her, and sends His Spirit to dwell within her, shaping her into a Christ-like servant, whose life, in the end, was characterized by love – love for her God and for others - a perfect circle.

"God will look to every soul like its first love, because He is its first love." [6]

I'm convinced Ellen's story has crucial elements making it powerful and gripping - making it extraordinary.

1. A Life of Faith
First, my mother and father cultivated a faith in God through scripture and prayer. My father, like Joshua of old, committed his family to love and serve the Lord.

"...as for me and my house, we will serve the Lord." Joshua 24:15

They began and ended the day with scripture. They hid God's Word in their hearts as the sun arced across the heavens. Thus, they were strengthened and fortified for the vicissitudes of the day. With their morning prayers they sought access to the treasures of God's mercies and blessings. Their evening prayers brought them back under their heavenly Father's wings for protection. Their devotions were their spiritual milk. They read the bible, discussed the bible, studied the bible, contemplated the bible, memorized the bible, and shared the bible until it was embedded in their hearts.

"Thy Word have I hid in mine heart; that I might not sin against Thee." Psalm 119:11

    My parents had an insatiable longing for God. My mother once recounted a near-drowning experience she had when swimming in Stony Lake, a small lake near Lake Michigan. She was wading, when suddenly she stepped off a sandbar and found herself, over her head, in deep water. My mother knew how to swim the side stroke, but for whatever reason, she maintained that she would have drowned if my brother, Wendell, had not spotted her struggling and pulled her to safety. My mother remembered the desperate feeling she experienced when she thought she was drowning and her intense need for air. At that moment she was focused totally on getting to the surface.
    I think my mother and father experienced that same intense need for God. They hungered and thirsted after righteousness and cultivated that need with a daily diet of scripture and prayer.

"As the hart after the water brooks, so panteth my soul after Thee, O God." Psalm 42:1

    Their faith was strong and as solid as a rock. My mother is the only person I know who invited Jehovah's Witnesses and Mormon proselytizers into the house. She was so confident and open in her faith, she could listen to what they had to say without being defensive. When they were finished she would share with them her source of faith and hope. She never wavered or compromised her faith. Talking to them and witnessing only made her faith stronger.

My parents' faith deepened and intensified with life's experiences, giving them a living hope in the midst of their trials, disappointments, and sufferings.

"We can learn nothing of the gospel, except by feeling its truths." Charles Spurgeon [7]

At some point, when life was hard and the going tough, they learned how to view life in terms of eternity. Their faith enabled them to see past the cornfields, the cherry orchards, the clothesline, and the garden to see the life beyond. Their faith helped them through the disappointments of a blighted cherry crop, rotted potatoes, a diseased cow, and a sick child. Faith helped them to see, at the end of it all, their eternal inheritance.

In so doing, they came to see life from God's point of view. They became wise.

"The fear of the Lord is the beginning of wisdom." Psalm 110:10

"Hope is one of the theological virtues. This means that a continual looking forward to the eternal world is not, as some modern people think, a form of escapism or wishful thinking, but one of the things a Christian is meant to do. It does not mean that we are to leave the present world as it is. If you read history, you will find that the Christians who did most for the present world were just those who thought most of the next. It is since Christians have largely ceased to think of the other world that they have become so ineffective in this. Aim at heaven and you will get earth thrown in; aim at earth and you will get neither."[8]

Faith helped them when there was no visible answer to their prayers. According to Billy Graham, those whose prayers are not answered in the way they would choose, who hold on by faith alone, reap a far greater heavenly reward because they endure by faith and faith alone.

"Faith is what God asks of us. His invisibility is the test of faith. To know who sees Him, God makes Himself invisible." [9]

My parents passed the test of faith. They never allowed sufferings or disappointments to cloud their relationship with God but through faith and prayer, only drew closer to Him. They never forsook their Jesus.

Ellen's faith and trust in God saw her through the challenges of eking out a living on the farm and rearing her children. However, with the pain and loss she experienced with Judi's death, Randy's mysterious estrangement, loss of her beloved Henry, and her own declining health, her faith was strengthened. Through surrender and acceptance of the unacceptable she came face to face with the transience of the world of forms. She came to know a dimension beyond transient form, time, and mind where God exists. Suffering deepened and cemented her faith.

2. Suffering

I related earlier how my mother suffered with Judi through her prolonged depression and when Judi died, my mother in agony and grief, withdrew to her room, where she remained for a time, shrouded and alone.

How, a few days later, she emerged from her room, a changed person, still grieving but with a peace and serenity beyond understanding.

Upon reflection, I'm convinced she had a life-changing encounter with her God.

I picture my mother lying on her bed, facing the window, totally broken, at the end of her strength, her will, her hopes, and her dreams. All her attempts to help Judi had failed. Her prayers for healing had not been answered. Where was her God? Why had He not answered her prayers? Why had He not healed Judi? Why had He not removed the affliction from her? What would become of Judi's family? Her two young sons and husband? Why? Why?

"My God, my God, why hast Thou forsaken me? Why are Thou so far from helping me, and from the words of my roaring?" Psalm 22:1

Could it be that the "Why?" moments of our lives are such important crossroads because they are times when we either find God or forsake Him?

It is a poignant truth that greatness issues from suffering and despair. The greatest spirits, the most blessed lives, the beloved hymns, the haunting symphonies, the powerful tales -- all are created from pain and sorrow. Fanny Crosby might never have written her powerful arsenal of hymns if she had not been afflicted with blindness. Beethoven wrote his Ninth symphony when he was battling deafness, Van Gogh painted his masterpieces in the throes of depression and Handel wrote the Hallelujah Chorus when he was poverty stricken and suffering from paralysis.

Suffering is a given of the human condition -- the Christian term for the dysfunction inherent in humanity. To the Hindu it is called "maya," and to the Buddhist, "dukkha," but all refer to the same dysfunction.

According to Christian teachings, this state of dysfunction is one of "original sin." Eckhart Tolle suggests sin is a word which has been greatly misunderstood and misinterpreted.

"Literally translated from the ancient Greek in which the New Testament was written, 'to sin,' means to miss the mark; as an archer who misses the target, so, 'to sin' means to miss the point of human existence. It means to live unskillfully, blindly and thus to suffer and cause suffering."[10]

According to Tolle, this is the bad news; however, there is a second insight which is the good news: the possibility of a radical transformation of human consciousness, described by the Hindu as enlightenment, by the Buddhist as the end of suffering and in the teachings of Jesus, as salvation. Other terms for this transformation are liberation and awakening.

Fanny Crosby, Beethoven and Van Gogh, among countless others, must have experienced something of this transformation in order to have created their masterpieces. They experienced a shift in consciousness and in so doing, realized within themselves what all religions can only point to but can never name in words, because the experience transcends thought.

Likewise Ellen, a member of the organized church, in her time of suffering (maya, dukkha) came to know the difference between spirituality and religion - the difference between an inner realization and transformation and a belief system regarded as the absolute truth.

She had come to realize that how spiritual you are has nothing to do with what you believe but everything to do with your state of consciousness.[11]

I had always imagined God whispering to my mother as

she lay inert and silent in the quietness of her room, but when I realize the greatness that can come out of suffering if we but turn it over to God, I think C.S. Lewis's description is more apt:

"God whispers to us in our pleasures, speaks in our conscience, but shouts in our pains; it is His megaphone to rouse a deaf world." [12]

When Ellen accepted her suffering and anguish and gave it up to her Jesus, she found God anew and received a new heart and a new spirit with which to serve her God and Master.

The cross was central to my parents' faith. They believed that Jesus died on the cross for their sins; that the way of the cross was the only way to salvation.

"For God so loved the world that He gave His only begotten Son, that whosoever believeth in Him, should not perish, but have eternal life." John 3:16

In Ellen's "dark night of the soul," God, in His infinite compassion, found her at the cross. God communes most fully with us in our suffering because He too suffered when He gave up His only begotten Son to die on the cross for the sins of the world. It is in our suffering that we find the closest and deepest relationship with Him, if we but trust Him in our pain.

In the end, after all her questions, her doubts, and her fears, my mother laid it all to rest at the foot of the cross.

"...O my Father, if it be possible, let this cup pass from me; nevertheless, not as I will, but as Thou wilt." Matthew 26:39

She did not forsake her Jesus, even in her hour of deepest despair and blackness. Following the example of her Lord, through surrender and nonresistance to the circumstances of her life, her cross of pain and suffering was transmuted into salvation and resurrection. Yielded and vulnerable, she accepted the unacceptable and God wrapped her in His eternal Love and set His mark upon her.

Billy Graham describes God reaching into the world through miracles and the intangible blessings, which give His people the strength to outlast their sorrows. God works one miracle after another.

"God says, 'If you suffer, I'll give you the grace to go forward.'" [13]

"A new heart also will I give you, and a new spirit will I put within you, and I will take away the stony heart out of your flesh, and will give you a heart of flesh." Ezekiel 36:26

At the cross, God reveals His divine and eternal secrets, His pearls of wisdom. God never promised that our path would be smooth and free of pain but He promises to walk with us in the pain. The Scriptures clearly teach that affliction is a step in our full and complete development as children of God.

"For unto you it is given in the behalf of Christ, not only to believe on Him, but also to suffer for His sake." Philippians 1:29

Ellen faced her pain fully and emerged from the furnace of affliction more beautiful, Christ-like, and useful and thus came to experience joy and victory -- rewards given to those who trust completely in God.

"My brethren, count it all joy when ye fall into divers temptations;

Knowing this, that the trying of your faith worketh patience. But let patience have her perfect work, that ye may be perfect and entire, wanting nothing." James 1: 2-4

These mysteries can only be understood when we, like Ellen, have come into communion with God and set our sights beyond this world of pain and suffering, to life beyond, when we will be reunited with Him.

If we keep our sights focused on eternity, certainly we can suffer a few days here.

"...weeping may endure for a night, but joy cometh in the morning." Psalm 30:5

When Ellen emerged from her room that day, she wasn't singing and rejoicing, but she radiated an almost otherworldly calm and serene demeanor. Now I know why. She had not been alone in the room. She had been with her Lord the whole time.

When she emerged, her faith, exhibited in the crucible of suffering, was like a candle lit in the world of darkness, just as the cross is a symbol of hope and light to those who believe.

Life would never be the same for Ellen. Like Jacob of old, she had wrestled with her Lord and would forever bear the mark of her encounter — a broken, yielded, child of God.

By the grace of God, she accepted the necessity of self-sacrifice in living with suffering.

"Without your wounds, where would your power be?...The very angels of God in heaven cannot persuade the wretched and blundering children of earth as can one human being broken on the wheels of living. In love's service only wounded soldiers will do." [14]

In the soil of such a yielded heart, cultivated through devotion, bible reading, prayer, and a burning desire to know God and do His will, the Holy Spirit comes to dwell, finding favorable ground in which to produce fruit.

3. The Indwelling of the Holy Spirit

As my father plowed and tilled the soil, readying if for planting and my mother lovingly tended her roses, so my parents had prepared their hearts for the indwelling of the Spirit.

As they aged and matured, they exhibited patience, humility, forgiveness, understanding, unselfishness, kindness, gentleness, and love -- the fruits of the Spirit, wonderfully and visibly apparent. Though they had been through the furnace of suffering and affliction, their hearts remained sweet, humble, mellow and meek. It wasn't just that they had experienced times when they were broken and humbled. Their lives were clothed in humility.

"But the fruit of the Spirit is love, joy, peace, long-suffering, gentleness, goodness, faith, meekness, temperance..." Gal. 5: 22-23

My father was a meek and gentle man, not disposed to confrontation. In the face of an argument, especially a religious one, he would make his beliefs known and then quietly withdraw from the fray. His temper flared at times while we were growing up, but his anger had more to do with frustration and a feeling of inadequacy than a mean-spirited nature. Because of his mellow nature, the spirit's workings in my father weren't as dramatic as those wrought in my mother.

"Blessed are the meek for they shall inherit the earth." Matthew 5:5

    This is not to say my mother was not a nice pleasant person. But the truth is, in her early years on the farm she would probably not have been described as meek or even gentle.

    My mother was hardworking, independent, fiercely loyal to her beliefs and family values, cognizant of right and wrong, intelligent, uncompromising, talented, and creative -- perhaps, even a bit proud. In dealing with the hardships and challenges of the farm, she might have appeared almost stoical to an outsider -- calm and unflinching in the face of affliction and bad fortune. To some extent, my mother's strong character might have contributed to her inlaw's and Lena's seeming aloofness towards her. You remember, even though my mother was a farmwife -- Henry's farmwife, she was more than just a farmwife. Though all of this was at a subconscious level and not intentional by my mother, they may have mistook her strong, resilient attitude for a better-than-thou stance and resented Henry's "citified" wife and her presence on the farm, thinking her too dandyish for their tastes.

    Needless to say, then, my mother was not naturally meek, sweet, and gentle. She and Henry worked hard for what they had and when they were able to save up some money for themselves, my mother had good taste -- she grew up with money and she liked nice things. I remember visiting once, when my son, George was just a baby. After nursing, he upchucked his milk all over my parent's brand new sofa. There was a definite coolness in the atmosphere and I remember leaving rather abruptly.

    Many years later, when I was teaching school, I thought of this incident when I was visiting the farm on a field trip with my third graders. I had been coming to the farm regularly for a spring field trip. My mom, then living alone, looked forward to these visits. After our tour, she would bring her lawn chair outside and, with the children gathered around her, would tell stories of what life was like on the farm in the olden days. One year it rained. Not to be denied her time with the children, Ellen invited all sixty of them, along with the volunteers, into the dining room. "Shouldn't the children take off their shoes?" one of the more sensitive parents asked, as the children marched into the house, muddy wet boots and all. "Absolutely not," answered my mother, "children are more important than carpets any day." I couldn't help but remember the many times when it had mattered to her that we tracked in the house, forgetting to leave our shoes at the door.

The spirit's working in my mother was a wonderful phenomenon, because the smoothing out of the rough places and the straightening of the crooked ways, did not mean that she became weak, vacillating, compromising, or shilly-shallying. Not in the least.

She was absolutely tenacious and unyielding where her faith was concerned, yet her conversations were without judgment or ego. She was gentle as a lamb, but powerful as a lioness.

Her naturally strong nature, coupled with a brokenness and complete yieldedness to God's will, was transformed by the spirit into that of a suffering servant -- Christ-like, holy, and saintlike.

"Take my yoke upon you, and learn of me; for I am meek and lowly in heart..." Matthew 11:29

Completely controlled by the spirit within her, Ellen was reaping the unlimited benefits from God's storehouse, reserved for those who trust Him.

With the Spirit's help, she came to experience peace in the midst of troubles and in spite of suffering. So complete was her trust, she overcame worry and hopelessness.

"Be careful for nothing; but in every thing by prayers and supplication with thanksgiving let your requests be made known unto God. And the peace of God, which passeth all understanding, shall keep your hearts and your minds through Christ Jesus." Philippians 4:6-7

As Vance Havner, the old country preacher noted, "Worry is like sitting in a rocking chair. It will give you something to do, but it won't get you anywhere." [15]

Toward the end of her life, my mother exhibited an all-consuming longing to walk with Christ, to live for Him, and to please Him.

So great was her devotion, that every day, with her failing strength and waning body, she renewed her commitment to her Lord. She realized that we need to keep sin out of our lives so that the Spirit can produce His fruit in us.

"Relying on God has to begin all over again every day, as if nothing had yet been done." [16]

"And be not conformed to this world: but be ye transformed by the renewing of your mind, that ye may prove what is that good, and acceptable and perfect, will of God." Romans 12:2

4. Discipleship

Unlike the twelve disciples of old, who were sent *out* by Jesus into the towns and villages of Israel to heal the sick, cast out evil spirits and preach the gospel, Ellen was called by her Lord to *stay* home and fulfill His purpose for her there.

Her calling was more like the man healed of demons,

who asked Jesus if he could accompany Him on His travels, only to be told: "Go home to your family and tell them how much the Lord has done for you and how He has had mercy on you." (Mark 5:19)

Discipleship involves obeying the call of God wherever He sends us and whatever He asks us to do.

It seems wonderful, and yes, remarkable too, that while Ellen lived her whole (adult married) life with Henry on a small farm a mile and a half outside a small village, the influence and impact of her life would be felt far beyond the confines of this limited geographical area. She was like a pebble -- a gem, which is cast into the waters, creating ripples that spiral outward in ever widening circles farther than the eye can see.

It's been noted that those who do not try to seem more than they are, but are simply themselves, truly make a difference in the world. Whatever they do becomes empowered because it is in alignment with the purpose of the whole. Their influence goes far beyond what they do and their simple unassuming presence has a transforming effect on those with whom they come into contact. So it was with Ellen and Henry. So perfectly content were they in their place, it would be difficult to imagine either of them living anywhere else. Their spirits were one with the birds, the crickets, the frogs, the breeze -- the very soil itself.

It seemed fitting that they both died in their home, on the hill, on the farm they loved so dearly. Ellen, for her part, had always been thankful that Henry had never had to live out his days in a nursing home.

Once, in his latter years, when he was hospitalized, Henry became disoriented, confused, and agitated. His problems were physical ones but in his confused state we began to worry about his mind as well. Once, we watched him repeatedly lifting his arms upward, his hands clawing the air. We sang hymns hoping to calm his mind and spirit. He told us later that he was picking cherries. It seemed perfectly reasonable to him to be picking cherries from his hospital bed, so cleverly had his subconscious found something familiar and comforting to do in an unfamiliar setting.

The same was true for Ellen. After her stroke, she entered a skilled nursing facility for physical therapy and speech therapy.

She was not the same person away from her "place." I remember visiting her one day. She was not in her room so I went to the dining room to find her. The scene was heartbreaking. Here was my mother - my gregarious, talkative, and friendly mother, sitting at a table all by herself. My mother, ever the gracious hostess, who had prepared, served and hosted countless meals for friends and family, relegated to a table by herself, listlessly staring out into space, making a feeble attempt to eat her bland, tasteless food.

My brother, Wendell (who had promised his dad, Henry, many years before that he would always take care of Ellen), made the decision to bring her home and arrange for around the clock nursing care, if needed.

Ellen's mood perked up considerably when she arrived home. Though she was still physically challenged from her stroke, her spirits brightened and she became lucid once again. Of course. She was home, in her place.

It was as though away from their beloved farm, my parents lost their identity.

There are worse things than death after all. Yes, we grieved their deaths, but placing either of them in a nursing home would have been tragic.

In a sermon entitled, "Are You There?" Vance Havner emphasizes the importance of finding the place of God's will - being "there," where God calls us to be. He recounts the story of Elijah of old (I Kings 17:2-4,9,10), who was sent by God to the brook Cherith and the city Zarephath. It was "there," where God sent him, Elijah found the place of God's purpose.

The farm was Henry's "there;" the house on the hill was Ellen's Cherith and Zarephath. Dr. Havner notes "there" is not a particular emotional experience; it is simply the place of God's will.[17]

In their appointed place, like Elijah, my parents experienced God's blessing, His power, and His provision.

An old proverb states, "that where He guides, He provides," -- Ellen's mantra in the midst of hardship and trouble. She and Henry too would experience miracles of ravens and a meal barrel that provided nourishment each day -- enough to supply their needs, nothing more.

There on the farm where God placed her, Ellen learned the cost of discipleship, as described by Dietrich Bonhoeffer in his treatise, *The Cost of Discipleship.* He distinguishes between cheap grace, which we bestow on ourselves, and costly grace, "the gospel which must be sought again and again, the gift which must be asked for, the door at which {one} must know." [18]

Over the course of her lifetime, my mother resigned the rights to her own life, yielded up her will and let her Lord take charge.

She was "there."

5. "A New Heaven..."

Eckhart Tolle, in his book, "*A New Earth,"* describes

heaven not as a place but as an inner realm of consciousness. While this inner realm of consciousness was evident in Ellen, she very much believed that heaven was a place and longed for the time when she would go there to join her loved ones. Heaven was her ultimate, eternal destination.

I have described how, in the days prior to her death, my mother talked with Henry on her travels back and forth on the road to heaven. Upon reflection, the dramatic events surrounding her departure make more sense to me. I wonder if she was talking to my father because he had been sent back to accompany her to heaven at the time of her death.

According to Billy Graham, even though Jesus overcame death and the devil, we still need protection at the moment of death, when the spirit departs the body and moves through the atmosphere. Because the spirit of darkness lurks near the dying one, waiting for a final opportunity to pounce, God sends His angels to guard His loved ones and bring them safely home. [19]

Can you picture Ellen and Henry together again, their resurrected bodies, whole, glorified and strong, leading the victory procession? No wonder my mother was so anxious to die. Everything she had believed was now made evident. She has unraveled the mysteries of life that so befuddle and flummox us.

"Picture a piece of embroidery placed between you and God, with the right side up toward God. Man sees the loose, frayed ends; but God sees the pattern." [20]

Now, in heaven at last, Ellen sees the pattern also.
Transported from the house on the hill to the Holy City

with gates of pearl, streets paved with gold, and a river and tree of life.

"And he carried me away in the spirit to a great and high mountain, and shewed me that great city, the holy Jerusalem, descending out of heaven from God." Revelation 21:10

Once in a far off time and place, Ellen had processed down the aisle on the arm of her father, Benjamin, to wed Henry. Now she and Henry were together forever, in a city so beautiful, "like a bride adorned for her husband." Their golden anniversary, celebrating fifty years of marriage, wonderful though it was, could never compare with this.

In heaven with her heavenly Father and best Friend, her faith was finally made visible. Here there would be no sin, no sorrow, no pain, no suffering, no unrest. No crop failures, no blighted cherries no dry rotted potatoes, no money shortages, no sick children, no death or dying.

I like to imagine my mother in heaven. I'm certain she is using her many gifts to the fullest. She always accepted and embraced her role as a farmwife where God had placed her; yet her gifts overflowed well beyond the walls of the house, the rows of the garden and the pews in the church.

"...and his servants shall serve Him." Rev. 22:3

I know that my mother is in heaven with God. I believe that she is there interceding for those she loves.

"And another angel came and stood at the altar, having a golden censer; and there was given unto him much incense, that he should offer it with the prayers of all saints, upon the golden altar which was before the throne." Revelation 8:3

I picture her reunited with Henry, Judi, her parents, and

all those dear to her who have gone on before.

Now herein lies a dilemma; an enigma, I find extremely troublesome and one I cannot resolve. As far as we can tell, with our limited human knowledge and perspective, Judi, for all of her rigorous spiritual searching, did not come to accept Jesus as her Lord before she died; yet, how could heaven be "heaven" for my mother without her Judi – the daughter she loved, for whom she prayed unceasingly and for whom she would gladly have given her life? Indeed, separation from her Judi would be hell for my mother, not heaven, and I cannot think that they are not together somehow.

Erwin W. Lutzer, pastor of the Moody Church in Chicago, tells the story of a woman, who called in to his radio show asking if there was something she could do for her deceased, unbelieving father, "to get him out of where I think he probably went." Lutzer responds: "I have some good news and some bad news. First, the bad news: no, there is nothing you can do to change the eternal destiny of your father. The good news is that whatever God does will be just...not one single fact will be overlooked in judging your father's fate...there is no possibility that the information will be misinterpreted or that the penalty unfairly administered." He goes on to say, "And, yet, because they have come under the shelter of God's protection through Christ, they will be escorted into the heavenly gates." [21]

We must leave it in God's hands. Our heavenly father is both just and gracious. In that balance, I find hope and comfort.

6. A Serene Holy Life

When I think of my mother in her last years, I do not

think of her as infirm, frail or weak. I see a wrinkled, well-worn face creased with a smile of greeting. I remember a serene gentle person who radiated beauty and holiness. There was a vibrant peace and stillness about her though how stillness can display energy, I do not understand. I simply know it was so. There was no interruption or distortion blocking the light, which beamed from her countenance. She was transparent.

Eckhart Tolle suggests that ego - our false self, is what keeps us enslaved in dysfunction because we mistakenly believe that our minds and thoughts provide our identity. It is only when we realize the limitation of our thoughts and beliefs and cease equating our identity with them that we are free to realize the spiritual dimension that exists within each of us. In order to realize salvation (enlightenment, end of suffering), we must let go of ourselves - our thoughts, our beliefs, our ability to help ourselves, our wills - our egos. [22]

Through surrender and nonresistance to suffering, Ellen's ego was reduced, until finally, all of self had disappeared and was replaced with the spirit of God, so evident at the end of her life.

The holes left by pain were filled by the presence of God and the light of His presence obliterated her heavy time-bound self.

As she approached death, her inner nature became more real than her outward form - her tired, worn out body. It began to dawn on us that death is the end of illusion and nothing real will ever be lost.

There were other signs attesting to this transformation as well. Ellen became increasingly detached from her possessions and started giving her things away. She had accumulated many beautiful possessions in her lifetime, but her ego no longer was attached to things. Money became immaterial. Once, when the issue of money came up, she remarked, "I'll just sell a cow." She was completely non-defensive. She didn't need to be right; in fact she was very open to admitting her wrongs and mistakes - her jilting of Henry back when they were dating and her part in the cool relations that existed between her and Andrew, Jane and Lena. She was attuned to the simple, golden pleasures of friendships, family, and the beauty of nature.

When the weather permitted, she spent most of the waking hours of her latter years in a medical recliner on the front porch. Here she watched the sunsets and the birds and listened to the bullfrogs croaking and the crickets singing. Though she could no longer tend her flowers and her beloved roses, we brought them to her so she could enjoy their beauty and fragrance inside. How she loved the porch where she had sat so many hours with Henry! Starting in early spring, she would hold out for sitting on the porch 'til late fall, when the cool weather called for sweaters, afghans and a space heater.

Once, during the summer of her last year, she remarked that she couldn't bear to think of spending another winter inside. She died on September 1 that year and I've often wondered if she lost her will to live that summer. In the end, when your loved one refuses to eat, you can either feed them intravenously or respect their decision that "it's time."

By giving up self, she opened herself to the power of God's presence. She experienced salvation. She became good, something we can never achieve on our own.

The definition of a saint is one who is exceedingly loving, charitable, meek and patient; a holy, consecrated soul; one who has died and is with God; one capable of interceding for sinners -- that describes my mother. Like the saints, my mother had humble beginnings. Like them, she was human, but was touched by God in a special way. I like to think she was like St. Therese, who believed you could be ordinary, but that great love could somehow transform and transport you.

My mother chose to trust in God at every fork in the road of her life, when she had to decide between faith and doubt, acceptance and resignation, fear and hope. She never forsook her Jesus. Where faith was concerned, my mother just seemed to "get it," and her faith brought her home.

"Faith is the substance of things hoped for, the evidence of things not seen." Hebrews 11:1

Remember the busload of souls who went to heaven in C.S. Lewis's allegory, *The Great Divorce?* All but one chose to return to their former "Shadowlands," because they could not stand the brightness of the heavenly heights.

The one who remained would be my mother. Every difficult choice she had made readied her eyes for the light. Though the heavenly heights may have taken her breath away, she was prepared for the spiritual altitude.

Here, then, is the essence of my mother's life:

"Next to the might of God, the serene beauty of a holy life is the most powerful influence for good in the world." [23]

In closing, I should explain that I wanted to call this book, "My Mother – An Extraordinary Woman, An Extraordinary Life," because I truly think she was extraordinary. According to C.S. Lewis,

"Every human being is in the process of becoming a noble being, noble beyond imagination. Or else, alas, a vile being beyond redemption....There are no ordinary people...It is immortals whom we joke with, work with, marry, snub and exploit—immortal horrors or everlasting splendors." [24]

I believe that is true, but I didn't use the term, extraordinary or noble for my mother because I knew it would have made her feel uncomfortable. She never thought of herself as anything other than an ordinary woman of faith, who loved and served her Lord; however, her life is a testimony to what God can perform when an ordinary person, like my mother, is absolutely dependent and yielded to Him. That is what is extraordinary and it can only come from God. All of God, none of self. That use of the word, extraordinary, my mother would like. The beauty of her story, is that what God did in her life, He can and will do for anyone who asks Him – for you.

♥

Memories of Loved Ones

a memoir - "...a reflective rearrangement of actual events."
(Larry Woiwode, *What I Think I Did*)

Note: The truth of Larry Woiwode's description became clearer and clearer to me as I wrote my mother's story. *So this is what I've been about,* I thought.

I have no illusions that my reflection and rearrangement of the actual events of my mother's life is the only story that could be written about her. With seven children in our family, there could be seven memoirs and though each one would be different, each would be authentic.

Having said that, it is my hope and prayer that upon reading this memoir, those who knew Ellen will be able to say, "Yes. That's my mother! That's my grandmother! That's my Aunt Ellen! That's my friend."

In the end, even though my siblings spent much time helping me wean and sort out the facts of our parents' lives, this book is still written from my perspective.

In an attempt to capture the broadest, most complete picture of our mother, my brothers and sisters agreed to share their memories of growing up on the farm. Ellen's grandchildren and her caregivers were invited to share their memories as well.

As you read these reflections, the differences in the relationships between Ellen and her children and Ellen and her grandchildren will become apparent, as any parent, who is also a grandparent, has experienced.

As a parent, Ellen was responsible for her children's physical as well as emotional, psychological, and spiritual needs. In reflecting on our childhoods, any one of us, children, might wish wistfully, and perhaps somewhat selfishly, that we had had more time to spend with our mother - going for walks to the woods, reading books together at bedtime, skipping through the daisies together - time just "to be". But, upon reflection, each of us understands that life was extremely busy and challenging back then. There wasn't always time, after fixing the meals, picking the vegetables, doing the washing and ironing and multiple other tasks, for walks to the woods, reading books before bedtime and skipping. Yet our mother was always there.

In the grandchildren's memories, we catch something of the freedom of detachment that a grandparent has with their grandchildren. They enjoy them but they are not responsible for them. As one grandparent so aptly stated, "I can always give them back." In her latter years, with the challenges of eking out a living, daily chores and running a household of nine behind her, Ellen had time to relax and enjoy life with her children and her grandchildren. The grandchildren's memories attest to the wonderful relationships Ellen enjoyed with them.

"Her children arise up and call her blessed..." Proverbs 31:28

The Children Remember

Marilyn (VanGunst) Wassink

Marilyn Wassink graduated from Calvin College and taught for several years in the Grosse Pointe Christian School. While living in Detroit, she met Jerome Wassink, a medical student at Wayne State University. They married in 1962 and moved to Grand Rapids, Michigan, where Jerome did his internship at Butterworth Hospital. Upon completion of his internship, they moved to Holland, Mi, where he joined a family practice group (Holland Family Medicine) and worked at Holland Hospital. He practiced for 35 years before retiring but continued as medical director of Hospice for several more years. Marilyn taught preschool in Holland for several years. They enjoy spending time with their three children and seven grandchildren, reading, gardening, and playing bridge.

Thinking back on my childhood has been an interesting experience - growing up as the oldest of seven children on a farm about one and a half miles from the town of New Era, Michigan.

Early on we had no telephone, but occasionally someone would call for us to our grandparents (my dad's parents), who lived next door and we would answer on their phone. We had no automatic washer or dryer - clothes were hung outside or in the basement during bad weather. We had no TV so in our spare time we played games, listened to the radio or read books.

My aunt {Lena} lived with our grandparents and she would give us piano lessons. We had no regular schedule but she would call to say that one of us could come that night for a lesson. There was some scrambling about then to see who might be ready! I remember sometimes after a lesson my grandparents would join in for a game of Hide the Thimble. I have played this with my grandchildren as well.

We often rode to school with our aunt {Lena}, who worked in a grocery store in town. She would sometimes have to wait (not too patiently) for us. One day Wendy came running out to the house, fell on his syrup pail, which carried his lunch and had the wind knocked out of him. Those of us already in the car were so scared for him, we set up quite a crying!

Canning and freezing kept Mom busy during the growing season. She always had a garden, both vegetable and flowers, strawberries and raspberries. Mom loved roses and she often ordered new bushes from Jackson and Perkins catalogues. She knew the names of each and Dad would help by dusting them. She loved bouquets of flowers in the house.

While the boys had chores in the barn and around the farm, we, girls, had our tasks in the house. Saturday was often baking day - cakes, pies and Mom's wonderful bread and cinnamon rolls. We took turns washing the dishes and our claim to fame was how high we could stack them in the sink to dry! When it was our turn to wash a canned meat jar, we had to spend extra time getting every little speck of meat out!

Picking cherries and asparagus were part of our summer - we were paid according to the amount picked and we were very competitive! Later on I "graduated" to a job at the grocery store in New Era.

Keeping us all fed was a challenge for Mom - her weekly grocery budget was rather small but there was milk from the cows, eggs from the chickens, produce from the garden and meat available. During strawberry season, we loved the shortcake with homemade biscuits and the wonderful Dunlap berries - topped with lots of whipped cream!

Dinner was followed by a bible story, prayer (both before and after) and a recounting of the day's events.

Church services, Sunday School and catechism were a regular part of our week. Mom went to the Ladies Society meetings (and often led them), while Dad served on the consistory. They often had company on Sunday evenings and sometimes we were included for a hymn sing, followed by lunch. Mom loved to play the piano and later she took up organ playing. She and Dad would occasionally sing duets.

Rog and Wendy pitched a tent one evening, intending to "camp out." Judi and I decided to have a little fun and made some noise outside their tent. They went running into the house, sure that there was an animal out there. Even to this day they deny that they were frightened but we had witnesses!

Mom and Dad began attending the Winona Lake Bible Conference for a few days each summer and they were blessed by the speakers and by the people they met. The boys stayed on the farm and we girls stayed in town with our grandparents. This was a treat because we could walk to the ice cream store and I'm sure our grandparents spoiled us a little! Sometimes our cousins would join us and they added to our fun.

There was sadness in our family with our sister, Judi died and our brother, Randy left home. Mom and Dad's strong faith helped them through these times. Mom never gave up on Randy - she kept sending him birthday and Christmas remembrances, even though he did not respond to her.

Her faith in God, her positive attitude and her love of

family and friends are inspiring to me. Hardly a day goes by that I am not reminded in some way of her love. Both Mom and Dad have left us a legacy of faith and love and for that, I am grateful.

Henry VanGunst

To have a special bond with nature is a unique joy in life. When I reflect on the experiences I have shared with my father-in-law, Henry VanGunst, I treasure the moments spent with him in this communion with the beauty of the Earth.

Whether our visits to the farm were in winter or summer, Dad always enjoyed the sunsets viewed from his home. He would remark on the changes in the vistas of the sunset with each season, another marker of the passage of time.

When traveling with Mom and Dad to Gordon's Lodge on Manitoulin Island via ferry, we were remarking on the loveliness of the sunset views over the bay. Dad agreed with our statements but added there was nothing as beautiful to him as sunsets over the rolling hills and varying landscapes, as seen from the farm.

Although Dad enjoyed the bay and Lake Michigan, he was truly a man of the land. The image of Dad plowing fields while riding behind a favorite work horse, listening to the birds, and singing hymns, describes Dad as a person completely in tune with nature and the land, on a plane that my generation rarely achieves. I see this respect and love of the land reflected in Roger and in my children and I am thankful for this gift given by Henry VanGunst.

Wendell VanGunst

I was born on this farm and have lived and worked here most of my life. I spent two years at Michigan State University in the field of Dairy Science and two years in the Army with the military police. In 1964 I returned from the army and married Ruth Fisher from Muskegon she was a graduate of Blodgett nursing school and is a registered nurse. We have four children together. We started what is now Country dairy and all our children in one way or another have been involved in the farm. Our family home was the home of my grandparents Andrew and Jane VanGunst who started the farm here when they married. The farm continues with another generation and we all affirm that God has indeed been good to us.

If I could sit today with Mom and Dad the thing I would most want to say is, "thank you". It was my unique privilege to know them as parents, next door neighbors and business partners. I worked with Dad most of my life. As parents they gave me a childhood I will always remember with great fondness. While not rich by some standards the home I remember was one I certainly cherish with many fond memories. In spite of having seven children, they somehow found time for picnics at a little park on the way to Ludington and many visits to the area beaches. We played ball in the pasture, sailed on the pond in the sap pan, made maple syrup in the woods, built our own ski jumps and made our own toboggan, went black berry picking in the woods and took many Sunday afternoon walks in the woods looking for wild flowers. We ate meals together around a table and always had enough to eat and clean clothes to wear. We also learned how to work, picking up stones, milking cows by hand (squirting the cats), raising ducks to sell at the farmers market, eating dinner with the threshing crews, tormenting the cherry pickers, picking up potatoes in the fall and sorting potatoes in the old cellar in the winter. I still remember Dad and my Grandpa discussing Dr Barnhouse's latest sermon, which they had heard on the radio. I really only spent about five years off this farm. When I returned from the military in 1964 I married Ruth Fisher and from then until their death we lived next door to Mom and Dad. I cannot remember ever having a dispute with them . We spent so many evenings walking up to their house and visiting. Invariably they were in the midst of reading and we would end up discussing some subject Dad was reading from Vance Havner or Dr Martin Lloyd Jones. Mom would insist on a dish of ice cream or a piece of fresh bread. Dad and I farmed together for about four years before he sold the farm to Ruth and me. I will always be thankful that dad was willing to mortgage all he had to get us started. Without that my dream of owning and operating a dairy farm may never have happened. Perhaps most important to me today was the faith they passed on to me and my family. They lived their faith each day. I will always be grateful for the relationship Ruth and my Mom had. Ruth became like a real daughter to her and mom became the mom Ruth missed growing up as her Mom passed away when Ruth was in college. If it had not been for the close relationship they had I believe keeping Mom at home until she died would have been very difficult. Church was always a part of the family I grew up in but we were taught it was okay to question and search out how our faith should impact our lives. I always remember their summer trip to Winona Lake Bible Conference near Warsaw, IN and how they came back so energized. My children were certainly influenced by the faith of Mom and Dad (their grandparents) as they fed the calves with Grandpa and often stayed at their home when we were gone. The last years of both their lives were not easy but I never sensed that they feared death - instead they welcomed it in the end. They truly believed and looked forward to a life that would be even better than sitting on the front porch they loved so much. I remember Dad calling me late one night from a hospital bed wanting me to come. When I arrived he wanted to tell me two things. One was would I promise to take care of Mom when he was gone which I assured him our family would do. The second was to apologize for not being able to give more to his family. I shared with him then as I feel now that no parents could have done more to provide happiness to their family and set a example of how to live life successfully. I will always be thankful for the home I grew up in and the parents God gave to me.

Ruth (Fisher) VanGunst

I became part of the VanGunst family on 8/14/1964 when Wendy and I were married and moved into the original farm house next to Henry and Ellen VanGunst-- Mom and Dad. I was warmly welcomed by all the family-- and living next door to Mom and Dad for 40+ years, we became very close. Over the years, there were lots of good memories. Our four girls were born and raised on the farm. They enjoyed spending time with both grandma and grandpa. There are still things that always remind me of the years with my very special neighbors!

Whenever I bake bread or rolls and use the stainless mixing bowl that was a gift from Mom, I remember all the rolls and breads she made. We always got a loaf of her raisin bread when she made it. (Sorry the rest of you missed out!) I have tried to make that bread, but even with her recipe, it won't raise for me! She taught me how to make many of the VanGunst favorites--Russian Fluff, Rhubarb Upside-down Cake, Shortcake, Peach Cobbler, and many more. She peeled peaches with me during canning time and showed me how to make pickled peaches and pears.

Each week when I do my Coffee Break Women's Bible study lesson, I remember the years we went every Tuesday morning together. Each Sunday morning, we would both pull out of the garage for church about the same time. Wendy has the Vance Havner devotional books that always remind me of the summer trips they took to Winona lake and the things they would have to share when they got home.

Around my house, many items are a continual reminder of Mom and Dad's legacy. The afghans that all of us have, the quilts that were embroidered and hand quilted, the table clothes that are almost too pretty to use. Our walls were painted by Dad and the garden planted and weeded by him, too. The hoe he always used is still in our garage with just half the handle and the blade worn to a graceful curve from all the weeds he hoed! I can still see them seated in the living room watching our little girls open their birthday and Christmas presents. For many years the girls "helped" Grandpa feed calves and when they started school he always said he didn't know how he could do it alone in the morning.

When we travel, I think of the trips they took--Florida, Europe, England, Hawaii, "out West", and "up north" for color tours. It was always an exciting day when they returned home.

The piano and music of course reminds me of Mom, too. Mom gave Amy her first lessons at age 4 and Mom and Dad made many trips to her the girls' choir and organ concerts.

I think of Mom when I do the crossword puzzles and watch the Jeopardy Quiz show and remember how she could answer all the questions! The Library reminds me of all the books I got for her in the later years. She said she always finished them just to say she had!

We have the Grandmother clock that sat in their dining room for so long--so each chime reminds me of all the good times, the valuable life lessons and loving lives that they shared with us. Our lives and our children's lives are much enriched by their Christian example through the years.

Mom's final days were not easy--but her faith always shone through. We read the entire book of Luke on the porch that last summer. When we were cleaning out the house, I found a song book that they had used when Mom and Dad sang together. It made me remember when I was standing by the bed in the living room and she was breathing her last breaths here on earth--but it was not the end! She was then experiencing what she and dad had sung together over the years. She was then experiencing what she had believed and lived all her life. One of the songs she and dad had sung was *Finally Home* by Don Wyrtzen:

Can you imagine stepping on shore and finding it heaven?
Can you imagine touching a hand and finding it God's?
Can you imagine breathing new air and finding it celestial?
Can you imagine waking in glory and finding it home?"

As one of Dad's favorite verses says, "However, to the one who does not work but trusts God who justifies the ungodly, their faith is credited as righteousness." Romans 4:5

Joan (VanGunst) Sikkenga

Note: Joan graduated from the Blodgett School of Nursing in Grand Rapids with an R.N. degree. She married Roger Sikkenga, and they have been blessed with 3 children; Dawn (Mark), Scott (Cheri), and Dean (Jessie), and 10 grandchildren. Rog was in Christian school administration all of his career, and served schools in Bradenton, Ft. Lauderdale, Birmingham (AL), Kalamazoo, Palos Heights (IL), and Fremont. Joan worked part-time in nursing during those years. After retirement in 2006, Rog and Joan volunteered in both Nigeria and Kenya, and hope to continue serving in the future as opportunities arise.

How to describe my childhood in 1-2 pages – Well, fun comes to mind, and safe, and I guess pretty wholesome and old-fashioned. I have good memories of growing up on the farm! I was number 5 out of 7 children, and I just remember always having someone to play with. In the summer it was softball games out in the pasture until it got dark, or sometimes Kick the Can, or Red Rover, and sometimes Judi and I would walk to town and play tennis on the tennis court there. Tennis could drag on forever, because neither of us wanted to quit if the other one was ahead, so we usually had to keep playing until we were tied..... In the winter we would go sledding, ice skating on the ponds, or build a snow fort. As we grew up, we were expected to do some chores on the farm. We all picked asparagus and cherries, and the money Dad paid us helped to buy our school clothes in the fall. Also the girls usually picked beans, and the boys picked pickles. The boys had to help with milking the cows twice a day, and the girls helped with household chores such as cleaning, ironing, etc. I have to say that on cold, wintry mornings when Dad would call upstairs to wake up Rog and Wendy to go out and milk, I was happy to be a girl! (of course, Rog didn't always answer the call either...) I don't remember thinking we were poor growing up. I guess I didn't have many clothes back then, and probably most of them were hand-me-downs from Marilyn and Judi, but I think the kids I went to school with were in the same boat, so I didn't notice. Our house was pretty cramped with 9 people in it, and I never had my own bedroom, but the house was filled with love. Back then we were usually all home for dinner, so 9 of us gathered around the table every night for a home-cooked meal. I have fond memories of warm rolls, hot bread just out of the oven, homemade pea soup, spaghetti, fudge, creampuffs, etc. etc. I'll never know how we all got ready for church in time on Sunday mornings with just one bathroom, but somehow we always seemed to make it. Faith for Mom and Dad wasn't just a Sunday thing, however. Thinking back to evenings spent at home, I can picture Dad sitting in his big chair reading a Vance Havner book while listening to a George Beverly Shea record, and I suppose Mom was mending someone's clothes when she finally got to sit down... Prayer and Bible reading were a big part of their lives, and both of them were very open and vocal about having to rely on God for everyday needs, and to get through tough times. I know Mom and Dad didn't have much money to spend on Christmas presents, but one Christmas was really special to me. Jan and I each got a doll (with a china face) with several outfits that Mom had made for them – one outfit was a satin wedding dress that I thought was just beautiful! How she had the time or energy to sew doll outfits after getting us all to bed at night is amazing to think about! I still smile when I see the Big Dipper or the Milky Way or Venus because I think of Dad looking up at the night sky and pointing out the different constellations, and I think how he watched the movement of the sun through the sky during the summer from his vantage point on the front porch. When I married Rog and we moved away to Florida and started raising our kids there, it was always such a treat for our children to come up to the farm and spend time with Mom and Dad during the summer. When Dad would pray at the table, he would always pray for their children and grandchildren, so we knew that whether we were up in Michigan or not they were remembering us and the rest of the family every day in their prayers. I believe that continued until Mom and Dad were both called Home. That's how I remember Mom and Dad – connected to God and to their family.

"When I call to remembrance the unfeigned faith that is in you, which dwelled first in your grandmother Lois and your mother Eunice and I am persuaded that in you also." II Timothy 1:5

The Grandchildren Remember

Lynne Vork, daughter of Marilyn (VanGunst) and Jerry Wassink -

I have many wonderful memories of Grandpa and Grandma VanGunst. When I was younger, I would spend a week staying at their house. I loved staying in the room upstairs. I would help Grandpa feed the calves with a bottle of milk. Grandma would make me a wonderful breakfast and those wonderful times sitting on the porch! They were truly a very special couple! I loved eating dinner at their house around their beautiful dining room table! Many games were played at this table.
 I feel very blessed to have had such wonderful grandparents in my life! I always enjoyed visiting with them. May their legacy live on forever!

Brent Sikkenga, son of Judi (VanGunst) and Wayne Sikkenga -

Reflections

My memories of Grandma VanGunst thread through the fabric of my earliest childhood and weave through the formative years of my early adulthood. Upon reflection I can see that much of my being has been molded by interaction with my grandparents, the comforting and serene haven of their home, the knowledge that they would happily welcome me anytime, the life grounding presence they provided, comforting advice, and most of all steady, unconditional love. Looking back through the winding and somewhat rocky path of my life I understand that much of my inner strength and motivation comes from the influence that they both had on my life. Unfortunately my time spent with grandma in the last years of her life was not as frequent as desired and became the occasional visit or phone call as life pulled me in other directions. I regret this, but feel that there was always an instant reconnection no matter how much time passed as there are some people in life who you can go significant amounts of time without communicating or seeing, but when you do it is like you saw them only a day or a week ago. Both grandma and grandpa were like this and always were welcoming without pressures of guilt and enjoyed any time spent with them.

Since my time was limited with grandma later in her life, my memories are less around specific events or stories and more around the essence of who she was and what she meant to me through the prism of my perspective and formative events in my life. To me grandma was a person of indomitable spirit, strong values and convictions, and an unwavering presence. She had a strength of personality that could be witnessed when she was involved in many of the heated political or world events debates held around her dining room table, barreling down the road well in excess of the speed limit, holding a conversation on the phone, meticulously tending to her rose beds, or trouncing someone in a game of pool in the basement. From a distance she could be seen as stern and possibly reserved, but upon closer interaction the stern demeanor was often found to be closely followed by a mischievous twinkle in her eyes and a playful laughter. However, that doesn't mean that I often tried to push past the limits of that twinkle and laughter to see what came beyond the stern disciplinarian persona as many stories had been ingested of the troubles my uncles had gotten into and certainly knew that I did not want to delve into the territories they had already tested!

Visiting my grandparents was always like going back to the center of my universe. It was warm and predictably comforting, a calming environment that rarely changed through the years, and peacefully tranquil. Conversations could be about personal challenges in life if desired, but both grandpa and grandma never pressured to know more or delve deeper than what was desired to share and often conversations revolved around stories about their memories, happenings at the farm, news events, or the storied tales of the troubles that Uncles Rog and Wendy usually got themselves into as kids. Sometimes sitting in the summertime shade of the porch with grandma or the late spring sun by the garden with grandpa could be spent with very little conversation as being in their presence was comfortable and they seemed to know that the shared personal time gave both parties further strength in our bonds.

The chance to go to grandma and grandpa's house

always felt like an opportunity to me and never a chore that had to be done. I always felt like I came away with something positive after a visit and grew a little bit more as a person. Even to this day I can relive going to their home to visit in my mind and it has a soothing and calming effect on me. It helps me to remember who I am and where I come from. I have inherited from my grandparents a sense of responsibility, willingness to work hard, a manner in which to conduct myself, a love of reading, music, travel, nature, the appreciation for simple pleasures in life, but with a refined desire to always learn more and expand my knowledge beyond my personal world.

A visit to grandpa and grandma's house brings back memories of the faint smell of a dairy farm on grandpa's clothes and the smell of homemade cooking in the warmth of grandma's kitchen. There is the sound of classical music and the grandfather clock, the sound of billiard balls clinking in the basement, buzz of conversation around the dining room table, and the chirping of birds outside by the flowers and birdfeeders. Memories abound with the smells of fresh baked bread, pumpkin pie, and the prized chance to sample some of grandma's amazing head cheese. Going back many years are the memories of lunch or dinner around the dining room table with Uncle Randy and hearing the passionate discussions and debates that usually resulted.

Any family gathering that occurred at our grandparent's home or at that of an aunt and uncle was an event to look forward to with much anticipation and excitement. There was the fun of seeing cousins again, playing games of Pit, football, basketball, or baseball with aunts and uncles, and seeing grandma and grandpa again while they revel in the middle of all the activity. Grandma was usually to be found voicing her opinions at the center of conversations, regaling with stories of the aunts and uncles growing up, or reinforcing our needs as children to be slightly mischievous.

While grandpa and grandma were deeply rooted and involved with the farm, family, local community, and church, these were not the limits of their horizons and they had a deep curiosity to learn more through reading, news, and travel. They traveled to other states to visit family or sightsee, visiting my parents when living in California and visiting our family again when we lived in Wyoming. I can still remember watching slides from their travels to Europe and being mesmerized by the adventure, discovery, and broadening of horizons that travel provided and it instilled a lifelong desire to experience for myself. Grandpa was kind, generous, steady, unflappable while grandma was outgoing, easily shared her opinions, the strong matriarchal personality of the family and they were both deeply loving and supportive of their family. I am sure that the inner strength and faith that guided grandma in her life were severely put to the test through events like Uncle Randy's moving away, my mother's untimely death, and grandpa's passing. Surely in private and confiding with her children these events were extremely difficult to bear and impacted her greatly, but from the perspective of a grandchild I am amazed and impressed that she showed such strength and composure to us while undoubtedly being torn apart inside. I think her faith was her rock through these times, but also knowing how she impacted and set the tone for those around her. Through these life-changing experiences she portrayed a steady resolve to accept what happened as being part of a larger plan and seemed to know that her strength was also needed by those around her to get them through.

I miss grandma and grandpa both dearly and reflection upon this now makes me understand how important they were in my life and in our entire family as a whole. They were the foundation for our family and the role models that I can only strive to emulate, but most certainly will never be able to match. I think as grandchildren we tend to look upon our grandparents with a certain level of reverence, but I do not think I could envision any way that they could have lived up to this any better.

Erik Sikkenga, son of Judi (VanGunst) and Wayne Sikkenga

These are the stories that I remember of Grandma. There was the time when George myself Andrea and Grandma. We were playing Phaze ten and I think we must have played an hour or more. I don't even remember who won. Another time Kristian and I and Grandma were taking a ride in the country around New Era. We were running out of gas, and Grandma said it was all right that her car had a spare gas tank, and not to worry. I honestly don't think that her car had another gas tank. I know Kristian and I felt a whole lot better when we made it to the gas station, and that we did not run out of gas.

Another time Grandma and I went out to eat at a restaurant called Fresh Catch. It was located in Hart Michigan We sat down to eat I think that I had water and Grandma had coffee We waited and waited for the waitress to take our order. So Grandma was getting impatient. So Grandma said that we were leaving. So we took off.

Grandma never paid for her coffee. I don't remember where we went after that. I was worried that someone would come after luckily that did not happed. I will never meet another person like Grandma she was one in a million. She told you like it was. She loved life to the fullest.

Amy VanGunst, daughter of Wendell and Ruth (Fisher) VanGunst

 I feel very blessed to have grown up next door to Grandma and Grandpa. There are so many memories that weave through my whole childhood and have so significantly shaped my life.
 Grandma and Grandpa were a part of our every day life. We walked up to borrow sugar, invite them to dinner, bring them their mail because their mail came in the same box as our mail, and to sneak a cookie from her corn cob cookie jar. I started piano lessons with Grandma when I was 4 years old and she gave birth to my on-going love of music. When I'm involved in a musical event, my mind often wanders to Grandma--thinking she's probably smiling as she listens from heaven. My piano lessons always ended with a game--usually a game of Yahtzee or Racko. Grandma didn't just let me win, however--her competitive streak made it a fair game, no doubt!
 Grandma was often outside when I was little. She worked in her rosebushes all the time. We were quite sure that Grandma wore shorts long before and long after my mom let us wear shorts. I still see she and Grandpa sitting in the lawn chairs in the south corner of their house where it was most often warm and sunny. And I can see her bundled up in her fur coat and hat, walking down from her house to the garage to go to church on Sunday morning in the middle of winter. In the last days of her life, in one of

our conversations, she asked me when her legs were going to start working again so she could get out in her garden. I told her that it wouldn't be long and they would work perfectly and I guessed that she would have a magnificent garden and lots of rose bushes. I'm not sure if she understood me, but I bet she did.

When mom and dad would go on a trip, we often stayed at Grandma's house. She would make Spaghetti or Rice and Raisins, usually bread, and always some kind of great dessert. I remember sleeping in the bedrooms upstairs--giggling quietly to avoid Grandma calling up the stairs. Grandma and Grandpa didn't have a television in those days--we often had to run back to our house to watch t.v. After they got their first television, with Grandma claiming all along that she didn't need it and probably wouldn't watch it, Grandma became and avid follower of Jeopardy. I can still see her sitting in a chair right up next to the television--I presume so she could hear it better. If I came up to visit, she would always turn it off, saying, "oh, I don't need that old thing on anyway."

Our family often enjoyed Sunday dinner at Grandma's. The menu was quite predictable: beef roast--or a special beef/pork roast she got from Cherry Hill--potatoes, creamed corn, salad, and home made rolls and pie. We ate dinner on the yellow rose china that sits in my china cabinet now. There was usually an aunt or uncle visiting as well and there was never a shortage of lively conversation-political, religious, or hysterically nostalgic-to entertain us. We were regularly regaled with the same stories from my dad and his siblings, although the version of the story changed depending on which aunt or uncle was relating it. The dinners worked out well for my sisters and I because, while we always made the obligatory offer to help with dishes, Grandma would always say, "oh, don't worry about that. Grandpa will help me with the dishes." She didn't have to tell us twice!

    I remember Grandma and Grandpa coming every year to watch us open Christmas presents or to celebrate our birthdays. In my high school years, I would frequently tell my mom after supper, "Mom, I'm going to walk up to Grandma and Grandpa's." I would walk up and walk in the back door--there was never a need to knock or ring the doorbell. I knew I was welcome. As I walked in, I would call out "hello!" and they would always call back telling me to come in. From spring through fall, I would usually find them on the sun porch--reading, crocheting, having devotions, or just talking. I would sit in one of the chairs and we would visit. In the winter, they would be sitting in the living room: Each in their own chair. We would talk about what was happening on the farm, what I was doing in school, what I was playing on the piano, their memories of my dad when he was young, church, community--there was never a lack of topics for conversation. I so enjoyed those evenings. When it got dark, I would get up to leave and give each of them a kiss before heading home--usually with a few things she wanted me to bring to mom and dad. When I came home from college, that was one of the first visits I made and one of the last I made before I left again. Grandma and Grandpa made several trips with mom and dad to Dordt College in Iowa for me and my sisters' choir and organ concerts. I remember walking with Grandma up to the big organ and letting her play it--she smiled from ear to ear! I always felt loved and supported by them.

    I remember the day that Grandpa died. Grandma's world changed forever that day. Her best friend and partner of 60+ years was gone. When I walked up to the house, Grandma walked right up to me and hugged me. I remember her saying through her tears, "If I hadn't loved him so much, I wouldn't be so sad. So, I guess it's a good thing I'm sad today."

I am so grateful that I moved back to New Era 5 years before Grandma died. I had the opportunity to be with Grandma through those years. I had the opportunity to take my children to see her sometimes daily. Her last months were hard, but I'm so glad I could be there with her. As she became less and less able to care for herself, I knew she was so ready to go to Heaven. I would sit with her and hold her hand and she would talk about Heaven--about how eager she was to see Grandpa again. Tears would come to my eyes so often. I remember her looking out the window from her hospital bed in the living room, and can remember her smiling at me. Her last morning, I stopped at her house on my way to work in Grand Rapids. It was early--maybe 6:30 am. We knew she the time would be short. I sat with her for a few minutes and listened to her shallow breaths. I prayed for her--told her I loved her. Before I left, my Aunt Joan, hugged me and said, "Amy, you know Grandma loved you." There was never a truer statement. I knew Grandma loved me--and all her children, grand children, and great grandchildren. A few house later, my mom left me a voicemail saying that Grandma's prayer had been answered and she had gone to Heaven.

There is nothing Grandma would want more than for us to share her solid and living faith in Jesus Christ. Her faith defined her life and her legacy. Her relationship with God was the thing that shaped her, helped her make her decisions, determined her priorities, and allowed her to love each of us. Grandma and Grandpa's life of faith in God left a powerful legacy in my life. I am so grateful for their commitment to Jesus Christ--it is that commitment that was passed on to my parents, then to me, and because of that, I am passing that on to my children. There is nothing more important than to teach our children about God and to bring them to a faith in Jesus Christ. Grandma and Grandpa did that--and I am so grateful for that gift. That faith in God sustained Grandma until the end and today I know she and Grandpa are living in the fullness of that glory in Heaven with God.

Dawn Feddema, daughter of Joan (VanGunst) and Roger Sikkenga

    As a busy mother of five, my days are filled with juggling schedules and trying to remember details. I have been known to rush upstairs to retrieve something important only to realize when I get there, that I can't remember why I went upstairs in the first place. It amazes me then, that I can remember details from my childhood with such clarity. Some of my favorite childhood memories occurred when our family made the long journey from South Florida to my grandparents' home in New Era to spend a couple of glorious weeks at the farm. My grandma, Ellen VanGunst, is a part of many of these wonderful memories. I can still hear her voice so clearly in my memory, see her busting around her kitchen and picture her cozy house just as it was the last time I was there.
    Many of my memories of Grandma involve delicious food - cinnamon rolls, homemade jams and pies, fresh vegetables and the best homemade raisin bread ever. My cousins and I would take a break from our adventures in the barn whenever we heard that Grandma had fresh-baked bread for us. The smell was heavenly and the taste of the warm bread with melted butter - mm!

My grandma was also a gifted piano and organ player. She used her gifts for many years at the church she and grandpa attended. As a little girl, I remember being amazed when I could hum a few bars of a song I'd learned in school and grandma could pick up and play the whole song without even having the music to look at! One of my favorite pictures is grandma sitting at the piano with my daughter Kaitlin sitting beside her, watching in awe as her grandmother played.

Grandma loved to feed and watch the birds at her many birdfeeders and her house was always filled with beautiful roses and plants. She created so many beautiful things for her children and grandchildren throughout her life - handmade afghans, intricate bedspreads, delicate snowflake ornaments for our Christmas trees. These things are all very special to me now knowing that they were created with love by the grandma I loved so much.

No visit to Grandma and Grandpa VanGunst's house was complete without a rousing game of Rook, Gin Rummy or Pit. Grandma loved to play games and she loved to win. I can remember the gleam in her eye when she'd pick up her hand and find the high and wild)Rook lurking there!

Grandma and Grandpa had a way of making everyone who visited them, feel welcome, cared for and special. From the warm hug at the door, to the table piled high with homemade food, to laughter as we played games, it was always fun to visit Grandma and Grandpa's house - even as an adult with children of my own. It was an awesome experience to introduce grandma and grandpa to my children - to feel the same warmth and love I'd always treasured, shared with my children as well. I treasure the many times we spent visiting on the back porch or in a shady spot in the front yard with grandma and grandpa throughout the years.

As I reflect on the lives of my grandparents, I am thankful for the countless memories of love and laughter that were a part of my experiences with them. I am thankful for the way they loved each other and their family and friends - for the love they lavished on me and my children. I am thankful for the heritage of faith in Christ that was the foundation for everything they said and did and for the way they passed that down to their children and grandchildren. I'm grateful for their example of Christian marriage and parenting that I now strive to emulate in my family.

As I remember Grandma, I can still see her striking white hair, lively brown eyes and ever-busy hands. I can hear echoes of her voice in the voice of my mother and I can see her fierce, competitive nature in my own daughter who bears her name. She set such an example for me as a wife and mother, who loved the Lord, her husband and her family. I'm so thankful for her influence in my life and for the precious memories that are mine. I miss her dearly and I look forward to seeing her again some day in Heaven!

Andrew Timmer, son of Janet (VanGunst) Hasselbring and Gary Timmer

I am never sure what is expected of these sorts of things. My memories of Grandma VanGunst are complicated. I remember a lot of darkness in the family, but I am not sure how much of that was real. I am learning that darkness and light are choices and that life is what you make of it.

Embrace what you love, and turn away from what you do not. At this stage of my life I associate Grandma with food, games, laughter, and peace. When I think of her I see her house, smell the farm, taste her food and hear her laugh. I see the view from her porch and swing. I remember the talks I had with her as a young adult, looking for my way. She was interested and thoughtful. Intelligent. I remember a coldness and reserve that came through at times when I was younger and which disappeared when Grandpa died. After he died, she seemed to relax. She was absolutely convinced that he was waiting for her in heaven. It was powerful. I remember how she became almost transparent as she neared the end. I remember feeding her in the hospital just before she died. She was a good lady. She improved with age and played a significant part in my life. The beautiful thing is that my mother reminds me more and more of her as we grow older and I watch her interact with my children. They are so alike. The zest for life. The interest in everything. The firm convictions that are still open to revision if new information becomes available.. I remember her fondly and am grateful to have had her in my life.

Annie Timmer, daughter of Janet (VanGunst) Hasselbring and Gary Timmer

My most vivid memories of Grandma VanGunst are summer visits to the farm. Each summer Andrew, George, and I would spend a week with Grandma and Grandpa. Our days were spent exploring the barns, chasing the cats, playing pool in the basement, walking to the big oak tree, driving to Fremont for mini-golf and lunch, sitting on the swing, playing in the yard, etc... My favorite meals were Grandma's cinnamon rolls and homemade spaghetti. At night we'd sit on the back porch playing greedy dice, Yahtzee, and Uno. I distinctly remember when Grandma taught me to shuffle cards the "adult" way – I was so proud! There was always the smell of fresh flowers (and cows) in the air. It was bittersweet when Mom came to pick us up, but we knew there would always be next year.

George Timmer son of Gary Timmer and Janet (VanGunst) Hasselbring

    In the summer of 2004, I visited Grandma for the first time without my family, when cousin Andrea was staying with her for a couple of weeks. I drove up from Grand Haven with the intention to visit them for one day; I had such a good time that stayed there 7 or 8 days over a two week period. There is a special quality to the memories I have from that time, in part because Andrea had a way of keeping a big smile on Grandma's face and in part because it was a time when I truly connected with Grandma and I came to know her better than I ever realized possible. I am grateful for that.
    I remember lazy afternoons on the screen porch, nestled in the shade and open to the breeze, watching the countryside and the cars that cut through it, appearing and disappearing in the distance. We would pass the time with mugs of tea and games of Quiddler and plenty of sitting quietly just enjoying the moment, inadvertently waiting for the old clock chime.
    I remember an evening when Uncle Wendy came over to be Grandma's partner in a game of Rook. Andrea and I were fairly reckless and carefree in our style of play, which induced plenty of "Oh my word," and "You're going to do *what!*" from Uncle Wendy and much laughter from Grandma. It's from that night that I can best picture her face.

I remember noticing the peace that Grandma had come to know. I had the sense that as her body faded, her spirit shined more brightly. I learned to see growing old as an opportunity and not as something to be feared—an opportunity to let go and love.

"Thus speaketh the Lord of hosts, saying, 'Execute true judgment, and shew compassion, every man to his brother.'" Zachariah 7:9

A Caregiver Remembers

Char Barnes, caregiver

It was summer when I came to the Country Dairy. Ellen VanGunst had suffered a stroke and was unable to walk. Immediately I knew she was very special. In my line of work, caring for the elderly, you get to know a person from the end of their life going back. Sometimes you don't have enough time to get to know very much. In this case I was blessed enough to share several months with Ellen in a beautiful place she had called home for many years, where she had raised her family, a place she loved very much.
Ellen was very quiet at first, not saying much, and never complaining. It was the family that told Ellen's story, not by words but by who they are, how they respected her, how they treated and cared for her every need and eventually how they shared memories with me about her. I learned how she loved the children and would read to them at the school, how she had been very active even in her late 80's. My favorite memories of Ellen were the times we spent out on the porch, the conversations, doing crossword puzzles (she always knew the answers), and having the pleasure of being able to read to Ellen. The book was by Walter Wangerin, Jr. titled The Book of God, The Bible as a

Novel. Over the summer we read almost the whole book. The best part were the conversations about what we read and listening to her thoughts about the things that I didn't understand. She was a grand lady and I was blessed just to know her.

In Ellen's own words...

The following poems, written by Ellen, describe her love of birds, flowers and the changing seasons. She submitted her poems to several periodicals and several were published.

Springtime Walk

I walked into a shaded woods
One balmy springtime day;
It could have been a land of dreams
I seemed far, far away.

All seemed serenely peaceful there,
I stopped and gazed awhile;
How good to leave the hurried world
And stroll this pleasant mile.

The flowers were blooming in beauty,
I picked trilliums of purest white;

I found them too, of deepest red
And adders tongues – to my delight!

What joy to pick a mixed bouquet
Some "boys and girls" with leaves of lace;
A jack-in-the-pulpit caught my eye,
So much to find in this lovely place.

Buttercups flourished in old creek bed
Their bright yellow blossoms were cheerful and gay;
There were violets of yellow and violets of blue;
And purple phlox in abundance to pick on the way.

The birds were singing everywhere,
Their happy carefree songs;
A flicker called out loud and clear
As through the woods I strolled along.

Fleeting Summer

It's sad to see the summer leave,
It's such a pleasant time.
The sunny days and balmy nights

Make living quite sublime!

There are so many birds around,
They sing so cheerfully;
They wake us in the early morn,
Then sing on endlessly.

In summer we enjoy the beach
And take the children there.
The water's fine; the sand is fun.
A time of leisure we share.

But soon, we know it will be fall
And summer fades away.
We must enjoy these lovely days
Ere winter comes to stay.

Let's listen to the birds' sweet song,
Let's visit the beach some more.
Let's watch the sunset over the lake;
What joys there are in store!

How fast the seasons come and go
The months go by in haste.
We must enjoy these summer days
Don't let them go to waste!

The Bird Feeder

It's time to feed our feathered friends;
Snow covers the ground once more.
So we have put our feeder out
With plenty of food in store.

The birds are wary for a while;
They hesitate nearby;
But soon they sense that all is well,
Their hunger bids them try.

The friendly chickadee stops by,
A small but trusting bird.
Next the nuthatch comes to share,
Then leaves to spread the word.

Ere long, we have a varied group,

Who are our guests each day.
The flashy cardinal with his mate
Decides there's food our way.

A flock of sparrows comes to call,
How soon the feed is gone!
A new supply we must bring out
Before the day is done.

The saucy blue jays, not afraid.
Will come to get their fill,
The feeder must be filled again
Before another meal.

We're glad to feed our feathered friends,
When winter comes our way
And we enjoy their coming
To our feeder day by day.

Christmas Greetings

It's time to get my card list out,
For Christmas time is here.

Our greetings are in order
To friends afar and near.

There are cards of all descriptions –
Gay poinsettias of brilliant red;
Others with the three wise men
Guided by the star o'er head.

Then there's the one of tradition
The partridge in the pear tree.
Some have jolly Santa Claus
With gifts for you and me.

The cards are truly beautiful;
The wishes are sincere.
It's a joy to send our Christmas cards
This merry time of year.

At least, I have them all addressed.
I've stamped them to be sure.
They're going to our many friends –
Some new and some of yore.

Merry Christmas and Happy New Year!
This is what our greetings say;
And we enjoy the greetings too
That come to us on Christmas Day.

♥

A Final Word

Author's Note: When I penned this letter to my mother, I did not plan to write about my dysfunctional childhood, but instead, set out to write about some of my childhood memories. Before long, however, the pen took over and forced the truth to be told. My letter is the result.

Dear Mom,
    a round, plump, black-capped chickadee sitting at my bird feeder...
    a bouquet of white, pink and purple peonies, orange nasturtiums or multicolored snapdragons...
    crickets chirping...
    a hymn sung or played on the piano...
    the aroma of freshly baked bread...
    tree frogs singing at nighttime...
    the fragrance of a rose...
    the feel of sand between my toes as I walk along the beach...
    a string of cultured pearls...
Any one of these experiences can trigger a memory of growing up on the farm.
    Playing hide-and-go-seek and Red Rover in the yard and baseball in the pasture among the cow pies...
    Going to Stony Lake or Lake Michigan when the chores were done...
    Picnicking at the roadside park just south of Ludington...

Praying and reading the bible with every meal and our discussions afterwards (I remember in one of our discussions, Rog became so animated, he picked up the jam jar and heaved it across the table to make his point.)...

Picking asparagus in the spring and cherries and beans in the summer...

Picking cherries was the hardest because, after picking the fruit at ground level, we had to maneuver the tall heavy ladders to reach the cherries higher up. We wore harnesses to which our pails were attached. Always competitive, we were constantly describing to one another how full our pails were: bottom thinly covered, bottom thickly covered, less than half, half, more than half, under the rim, even with the rim, above the rim, level full and heaping full. We worked hard to get the heap on the top, because two heaping pails would fill up one lug - the container used to transport the cherries to the cannery. If we hadn't been so concerned about how full our pails were, we probably could have picked a lot more cherries! We had contests, usually boys against girls, to see who could get the most lugs at the end of the day. I'm surprised we didn't have more accidents, when I think of us standing on the top of a 10 foot ladder, on tiptoe, straining to reach the cherries at the tip tops of the trees.

Dad was always there to encourage us and sometimes he'd pick along with us. You encouraged us, too, by fixing tasty mid-morning and mid-afternoon snacks which dad brought out to the orchard. The money we earned was used for school clothes and school supplies.

I remember the sad day when dad took our dog out to the woods and shot him because he had growled and snapped at one of us.

I don't remember much about dad's parents, Grandma

and Grandma VanGunst, who lived right next door, but I do remember your mom, Grandma Postema. Grandpa Postema died much too soon - before we really got to know him. We loved going to their big house in town, where you grew up. Sometimes we'd walk there from school and have lunch with grandma. In the summers we loved playing on her large screened-in porch. We'd visit her on Sunday nights after church and have dessert. She'd bake a cake and let us help pile on the whipped frosting. We stayed with Grandma when you and dad went away for a vacation in the summer. We slept in the bedrooms upstairs – there were four of them and they were large and roomy. I remember one had a pull-down door to the attic. Another had a huge Narnia-style wardrobe. I always felt a sense of mystery when we opened its doors. I loved Grandma. She was kind, big-hearted, and always seemed happy to have us around.

But, Mom, as I think about growing up, some troubling memories crowd in on my reverie.

I see a little girl standing alongside the road that ran in front of our house. Moments earlier, she left with her brothers and sisters to pick blackberries. But the others have left her behind and instead of running to catch up, she stands there. Frozen. Watching from the house, you, mom, call to her, to run and catch up with the others. That little girl wants so badly to go with them, but they've left her behind and seem to have forgotten about her. She wants - she *needs* for them to stop and notice that she's lagged behind. She wants them to come back for her, to wait for her, but the merry little band of berry pickers continues on, oblivious. And so she stands there, tears streaming down her cheeks, unable to move. You come to get her and take her home.

That little girl was me, crying out for attention, for someone to notice me, to show me that I mattered, to give me a sense of self; a center; an ego.

In that moment, in a little patch of gravel, alongside the road, trapped in my own little cosmic bubble, I experienced the universal human need to be loved, to be affirmed and understood.

That moment pretty much defines my childhood. I was a shy, withdrawn, introspective, and detached little girl. I'm sorry Mom, because with the challenges of raising seven children and tending the house and the garden, you certainly didn't need a problem child around.

But a problem I was from the very beginning it seems. Shortly after I was born, on November 10, 1944, dad came down with rheumatic fever. This must have been terribly frightening for you. Dad went into the hospital and when he returned, you nursed him back to health. During that time I cried so much you asked a neighbor to look after me. She became a kind of mother to me, but it was *you* I wanted to hold me; it was *you* I wanted to sing to me; it was *you* I wanted to rock me to sleep.

Shortly after dad recovered, you became pregnant with my younger brother, Randy. You were dangerously ill during that pregnancy and almost lost the baby. I don't know how you managed to keep up with the housework, fix meals and tend six children

I started school when I was four – too young it seems, because, everyday, when Mrs. Vanette, my kindergarten teacher, got out the marching band instruments, I started to cry. She would sigh and give that "Oh, not this again," look and my sister, Marilyn, would be summoned from her classroom to come march with me and stay until I stopped crying. So there I was, wailing away, marching around the room, beating my drum or shaking my tambourine, with Marilyn at my side. I'm sure she had better things to do. Because marching band was at the same time every day, she probably missed out on some crucial math or science teaching. Didn't they have school counselors back then? Someone to suggest that, perhaps I was not ready, emotionally, for school?

The day I had my tonsils removed, you told me we were going to the library. The first clue I had, that I wasn't going to be checking out any books was when I put on a funny-looking gown and got into a large, unfriendly-looking bed. The next thing I knew, a smelly cloth was placed over my mouth. I know now that it was a cloth soaked in chloroform, which was used back then to render patients unconscious, but what I remember, is four people in white gowns, each standing at a corner of the bed, smothering me with a sheet. I have been claustrophobic ever since. You were following a friend's advice in not telling me about my tonsillectomy and I know you felt sorry you hadn't told me the truth.

Remember those cute little black patent leather shoes you bought me? Well, those shoes were too small. They caused corns on my toes that are still there today. But I never told you the shoes were too small, so how were you to know?

Then, there was the time you and dad were enjoying an evening away together at Maranatha Bible Conference. Back at home, under the supervision of our older siblings, some of us, kids, organized a swing-jumping contest (where were those older siblings anyway?). Well, guess who won? Guess who broke her arm? You and dad had to come home early to bring me to the hospital, where I needed surgery to set my broken arm. On top of that, you and dad didn't have any insurance.

None could believe the height at which I jumped from the swing. Even I couldn't believe it! I scared myself. My impulsiveness revealed itself another time, when I was riding in the back of dad's pickup truck. As we passed the house, something inside of me yelled, "LEAP!" So I leaped from the truckbed, my spindly legs spinning and reeling in the gravel, where I landed in a heap alongside the road. I was badly banged up and bruised, but luckily had no broken bones.

Could anything else possibly go wrong?

I developed a sore on my leg, which turned into an ugly boil. One evening, while I was sitting too close to the rocking chair, the sharp end of the chair leg pierced the boil. Pus and fluid squirted everywhere. Back to the emergency room.

There was only one school where we grew up – New Era Public School. New Era had about 500 residents and three churches.

Our school was Christian in principle, if not in name. Every day started with a prayer and the pledge and every Friday we had an assembly, where we sang hymns, had prayer, and a devotional given by one of the town's pastors.

That all changed when the Christian Reformed Church decided to build their own school. Now there were two groups in town – heathens and Christians, based on where the children went to school. Guess which we were. That didn't seem fair. Even though our family still went to the same church as the "Christians," I felt ostracized at church, because we still went to the public school.

I wish I'd had a stronger self image, but remember I was the shy, introverted one. The Christian school kids made mincemeat out of me. Now, church, Sunday school, and catechism were added hellholes of anxiety for me. I sure surprised them one Christmas by reciting Matthew 2:1-12 for the Sunday School program. Reciting - by memory, no less! In truth, I surprised myself but, hey, everyone had a chance to tryout. Since I had no social life, I had plenty of time on my hands and memorizing bible verses gave me something to do.

You hadn't prepared me for the menses, and, when the time came, I thought I was bleeding to death. You felt badly I know because you hadn't explained it ahead of time to me.

I needed attention so badly, that one Sunday afternoon, when you and dad were having a nice peaceful drive in the country, I stole my sister, Joan's, necklace, took it apart and dropped the beads, one by one, down the register. To top it off, when Joan reported her necklace missing, I lied, claiming I knew nothing about it. My misdeed was so pathetic, it screamed, "Problem child!" I don't even think you punished me. You probably just felt sad and worried.

Getting attention, even if it was negative attention, was the reason I starting biting my nails. I remember you told me, if I bit my nails, they would never grow back again. I'm sure by this time you were at your wit's end and were willing to tell me anything to get me to stop. Of course, after you told me that, I kept on biting them just to see if what you said was true.

I was pretty much a loner throughout my childhood. How can you make friends when you don't have a clue who you are yourself? Things reached such a state in my teen years that I fashioned a world inside my head where I was important and loved. All I had to do was flip the switch and I was transported to a magical place where I was in the thick of the activity, popular, cool, and smart.

The more I lived in my make-believe world, the less I interacted in the real one.

I could take my world with me anywhere. When we traveled I only had to close my eyes and I was there. You told me once Mom, with some puzzlement, that I spent an entire trip to the Upper Peninsula in MI in the backseat, with my head under a blanket. You wondered what I was doing under there. Good thing I didn't try to explain that the blanket was only a prop for my imaginative world. I had a whole life going on under that blanket!

I was nervous when 10th graduation approached. My three older sisters had been valedictorians of their classes and I felt some pressure to uphold the family tradition. To accomplish this feat, I had to beat out the other students in my class – all five of them. This I managed to do. My accomplishment was tarnished slightly by the fact that I, compared to my sisters, had beaten out the fewest number of fellow students.

After graduating from the 10th grade in New Era Public School, I attended high school in Muskegon, MI, some forty-five minutes away. That summer, I pored over my sister Joan's high school yearbooks. I knew every student's name and face, but when I got there, I was too shy to meet any of them or make friends.

Yet another little flash of promise: Shortly after starting high school, I joined the choir. They already had an accompanist, but one day, the director, knowing that I, too, played the piano, introduced a Christmas piece with a difficult accompaniment – "For the Glory of the Lord," from *The Messiah*. She announced that whoever could play it would become the regular accompanist for the choir. I went home, practiced the piece, and won the audition a few days later. I surprised myself!

I graduated from high school and now, fast forwarding to adulthood, I graduated from college with a teaching degree, was married and had three amazing and beautiful children. I had pretty much left my make-believe world behind by now and was learning to navigate in a grown-up world of marriage, teaching, parenting and friendship.

During these years, my husband and I strayed into a liberal church, whose pastor, in an attempt to adapt the gospel to the modern mind, uprooted everything you and dad believed and had taught us. I am ashamed when I think of how I parroted the modernistic, flowery, theological gobbly-gook I heard from the pulpit and tried to undermine your traditional, literal views of the bible. You were always up for a strenuous discussion of theology, but Dad, though bright and well-read, was a simple man with a simple faith. He read and studied the bible daily and enriched his reading with books by spiritual giants of faith, Vance Havner, Donald Barnhouse, Billy Graham, Ironsides and Dwight L. Moody. He was not one to confront or argue. How contemptible it was for me to attack what was most precious to him - his faith. His faith had weathered the trials and rigors of life in the trenches, the death of his daughter and the estrangement of his son - it was the bedrock of his life.

Once after I had backed him into a corner on a biblical point, he remarked quietly " Well, I'm going to believe what the bible says." How sad he must have felt that his child, raised on a daily diet of bible reading and prayer, had gone so astray.

I remember once, discussing the noncanonical or gnostic gospels with you. You listened politely, as I described how these documents, discovered in upper Egypt in 1945, revealed startling information about the early church and the beginnings of Christian orthodoxy. I admit that I was trying to shock you with my newly acquired knowledge of how the early church was split from the beginning, how Jesus' followers didn't agree about the facts of His life, the meaning of His teachings or the form that the church should take. I guess I thought that what I had read about these gnostics might shake the foundation of your faith a bit - how they, like Matthew, Mark, Luke and John, wrote about Jesus' life on earth with His disciples, but maintained that self-knowledge is essentially knowledge of God; that Jesus, instead of coming to save us from sin, comes as a guide who opens the way to spiritual understanding and that when we recognize Him (as Thomas did after the resurrection), we become as He is - divine. I remember suggesting that it was politics and bullying tactics by those in power, such as Irenaeus, that determined which gospels were allowed into the bible and which were banned as heretical. I suppose I was attacking the bedrock of your faith that the bible is the inspired Word of God but you weren't even shocked by these revelations.

You listened with interest and then pointed out to me that the gnostics lived almost two hundred years after the time of Jesus, they usurped the names of the apostles to give their writings credibility and most disturbing of all, they believed one could find Jesus, by looking within one's self, instead of looking to the accounts of those who actually walked with Him. Totally non-defensive, you used our discussion as an opportunity to witness to your faith. It was hard to argue with such calm confidence. Even though you were loyal to the church as the imperfect body of Christ here on earth, it was obvious that your faith was bigger than what was contained and taught within its four walls. When you talked about your faith, it was as though you possessed secret knowledge that gave you incredible peace and serenity.

Sadly, I didn't enjoy a close relationship with you or dad during those years. I don't think I was especially pleasant to be around - a know-it-all impressed with myself and my modern ideas. I didn't think I needed you and dad in my life. Thinking back on those years, I think I resented you for my unhappy childhood and the lack of bonding between us. That needy little girl had grown up but she was still there, longing to be important, wanting to be loved and understood, not just by anybody, but by the person everyone must bond with if they are to be well-adjusted, contented, loving people – their mothers. During this time Judi's depression deepened and Randy became estranged from our family.

You had so much to deal with, Mom, you may not even have been aware that I longed to be close to you, but instead, I turned away, pretending that it didn't matter. My resentment and bitterness only hurt me.

Then, in an epiphany moment, I realized that I had been viewing myself as a victim of my childhood. When I changed my perspective and viewed events from your perspective, I came to understand and appreciate everything you had to deal with while I was growing up. I realized that you did the best you could. And even though my dysfunction and unhappiness weren't your fault, I forgave you for all the bad things that happened, just the same. When I no longer thought about myself, but thought about you and your wellbeing, the resentment and bitterness suddenly disappeared. Gone was the burden I had carried around. The past no longer had a hold on me. I was free.

During these years I went through a painful divorce and subsequent depression. I became so despondent and devoid of hope and direction, that, like Judi, I came to the end of myself. How I grieve to think of the pain and anguish I caused my children, you, and others during those dark hellish days. You must have had haunting flashbacks of Judi. I know you prayed for my recovery, and your prayers were answered. My recovery was nothing short of a miracle.

"Likewise the Spirit also helpeth our infirmities: for we know not what we should pray for as we ought: but the Spirit itself maketh intercession for us with groanings which cannot be uttered." Romans 8:26

Every time I visit Judi's grave, I realize, that, but for the grace of God, her grave could be mine. I can only weep.

Then, dad died and you were alone. I began spending more time with you, experiencing the mother-daughter relationship and the friendship I had never known.

You were so happy for me when I met Don. When we discussed marriage, I shared with you my concerns that Don was not a believer - an agnostic, perhaps, but not a believer. I asked you for advice. I knew there was a verse in the bible somewhere that stated, "...be ye not unequally yoked...." I was expecting you to quote that verse and caution me against marriage, but your response absolutely blew me away. You quoted a verse I had never heard of - words to the effect that I shouldn't worry, for God, in His justice, mercy and grace would take into account the fact that Don was married to a believer. You assured me that I should marry Don and leave it in God's hands.

I was blown away. I have never found the verse you quoted in the bible. I'm not sure it exists. And, now as I contemplate your words, I have come to realize that you were so determined that I should have a second chance at happiness, you made up a verse to erase my anxieties and uncertainties. She didn't just give me your personal opinion - you *made up a verse from the bible* - well perhaps, you paraphrased or altered an existing verse - to calm my uncertainty.

In thinking back on this episode, I am a little perplexed and greatly amazed. What you did that day was wonderful. I don't think, for a moment, that because you quoted a pseudo bible verse to allay my fears, that Don will automatically become a believer.

You knew your scripture. You were always strict about your beliefs and didn't cut people much slack. So, what were you doing, giving Don and me your blessing and spiritual reassurance besides? What can this mean? It's almost worth a chuckle to think of you rattling off a verse that didn't even exist! I can only deduce though, that your love for me was so great, it outweighed your knowledge and belief of scripture.

I don't believe you ever compromised your faith. I don't think you did with me. I can only wonder, if, for you, in the end, all was of Love, just as it had been for you in the beginning and throughout your life. Knowing how important it was for me to have a healthy relationship, after suffering so much dysfunction, you chose love and left the rest to God.

This is powerful. For me it demonstrates how strong and close your relationship was with God - a relationship that surpasses human finiteness and understanding. In that encounter, you taught me always to make the choice for love.

Then, in your last years, when you were homebound, I came home once a week with Max, my yellow Labrador retriever, to spend time with you. These days would become the most important days of my life. You became such a dear person to me. I had always loved you - you were my mother after all, but in those times, I came to love you anew.

I would arrive on my scheduled day with Max, who you adored. We'd chat for a bit, then you'd ask, "Shall we play Scrabble or Chess?" and our day would begin. I'd spend the day chatting with you, playing games, having lunch, reading aloud, playing the piano, or just being there. Max provided the therapy.

You loved Max, I knew. He'd grab your slipper or a dish towel, wanting to play. Once he lifted his leg and peed by one of your tall houseplants. Years earlier, you would have been annoyed and rightly so. Now you just smiled.

Max had been a Paws With a Cause foster puppy the previous year. I was to provide socialization and basic obedience training, then return him to the center where more intensive training would prepare him to be a working dog for the physically and hearing challenged. I had grown so attached to Max, I was torn when my year with him was up and it was time for me to return him to the center. Part of me wanted him to become a great service dog, but the other part, the larger part, was hoping that he would fail the training so I could get him back. I didn't know then that you had weighed in on the situation.

After a week, I received the phone call I was waiting for. Max was considered too aggressive for their program. Did I want him back? *Did I want him back?*

Before heading for the car to pick him up, I called you to share the good news. You were overjoyed. "I've been praying for this," you confessed. That blew me away. I knew that you had an "in" with God and that He cared about sparrows, but getting Max back for me? Wow!

After that, I had Max certified as a therapy dog. I like to think that he did his best therapy work with you.

Max and I stayed overnight with you shortly before you died. We were sleeping in the living room with you. Max heard a noise in the night and starting barking. You had not spoken at all that day, but I heard you call out in a weak, shaky voice, "Oh Max..." Those were the last words I would hear you speak.

And here is the miracle and magic of those days. I got to come home, to the house where I had been raised, to the farm where I had grown up, to spend time with you. Yes, I was an adult child now, married and a mother myself, but it didn't matter.

Together, we reclaimed what I never known as a child. The truth was, you had so many concerns, you didn't have time for the one on one relationship I so craved. I had gotten lost in the shuffle of a big family. That wasn't your fault. Because I hadn't bonded with you as a baby, my craving for love and attention manifested itself in dysfunctional behavior.

But, during our time together, the past dissolved. Those days were times of healing and redemption for me - for both of us.

God is good. He gave me time to enjoy what I had missed – time just to be with you. Those were moments of presence, of awareness - of eternity, and because nothing real is never lost, they are with me still.

"When, except in the present, can the Eternal be met?" [1] C.S. Lewis (Christian Reflections)

Here is the amazing thing. Though we were limited to the house, often the porch, where you spent most of the day, confined to your chair, there was a spaciousness to our time together that that was freeing, liberating. Perhaps the physical constraints forced us to narrow our focus to the present, into the world of consciousness and Being - the only place we can meet God. Is this what Jesus meant when he talked about entering "the narrow gate?"

It wasn't just the close proximity of space that gave our time together such presence. It was the very tangible sense of surrender that pervaded the atmosphere in the house. To be with you was to be in the presence of one, who, in perfect childlike trust, offered no vestige of resistance to life. You had no agenda other than just "to be." Is this why Jesus said, "Look at the lilies, how they grow; they neither toil nor spin?"

You were like a lake, which is still and serene at its depths, though ripples and storms might beset its surface. You were both absolutely vulnerable and utterly invincible.

In those days of wonderment, I met God. I had come to know Him through the revelation of His Word and in creation. And, then, in the times I spent with you, I found God anew. I looked in your face and saw Him.

In a flashback, I remembered something those pesky gnostics had claimed about the unity of the human and the divine. Not that it really mattered anymore, but, in the *Gospel of Thomas,* the gnostic, Thomas relates what Jesus said to him, after he recognized his Lord:

Jesus said, "I am not your master. Because you have drunk, you have become drunk from the bubbling stream which I have measured out...{She} who will drink from my mouth will become as I am: I myself shall become {she}, and the things that are hidden will be revealed to {her}." [2]

And this from doubting Thomas (although now I had to wonder about the name) - still, he could have made a believer out of me.

That's why mom, because of those days we had together, I can write about the bad along with the good. As difficult as my childhood was, none of it matters anymore. I made mistakes raising my children, and they probably stem, in part, from my own childhood. I've always believed that my children are the amazing people they are *in spite of me* not because of me. I always loved them - I just made some poor choices. But, I've come to realize that the pain has to stop somewhere. While it cannot be erased by ignoring or repressing the past, if we name the pain, it can be redeemed and forgiven through the power of Love.

The God of Love, who brings us into being, loves us even though we stray and wander off into our own little deserts of hurt, dysfunction and misunderstanding. He never lets us go. Through the power of love, He heals our brokenness. He redeems the bad and makes it good.

When you died, mom, it was Love that brought you home. I like to think that, one day, when God calls me to Himself, I will get to come home once again to see you – this time for eternity.

Your loving daughter,
Janet Lynne

APPENDIX – An Invitation

This tribute to my mother would not be complete without an invitation, to come to know the God whom she loved and served – the One who made her life extraordinary:

1. My mother loved traveling, but on the most important trip of her life, she never left home. That trip was down the Roman Road. You can make this journey too.

   "The series of verses {in Romans} summarize everything we need to tell others about how to receive Christ as Savior." [1]

   a. "For all have sinned, and come short of the glory of God." Romans 3:23

   "We can never be reconciled to God by trying to live a good life, for we are intrinsically, internally sinful; and nothing can exist in the blazing holiness of God's presence and perfection. Only when we realize this can we fully appreciate what Christ has done for us." [2]

   b. "The wages of sin is death: but the gift of God is eternal life through Jesus Christ our Lord." Romans 6:23

   "It's a gift that only comes wrapped in one package – Jesus Christ our Lord! Think of a great canyon. We're on one side in a state of sin and death; God is on the other side with the gift of eternal life. The cross of Jesus Christ is the bridge that spans that situation." [3]

c. "But God commendeth His love toward us, in that, while we were yet sinners, Christ died for us." Romans 5:8

"Never did four short words hold a bigger or better message." [4]

d. "That if thou shalt confess with thy mouth the Lord Jesus, and shalt believe in thine heart that God hath raised Him from the dead, thou shalt be saved. For with the heart man believeth unto righteousness; and with the mouth confession is made unto salvation." Romans 10:9-10

"...notice that both verses speak of twin actions that enable us to claim salvation. We believe with our hearts and confess with our mouths." [5]

My mother believed these verses with all her heart. Scripture was the ultimate authority for her, yet, toward the end of her life, her faith was distilled into a few simple truths. She would have agreed with the country preacher, Vance Havner, when he described his faith journey:

"There are a 'few things for certain' which I believe with all my heart. There is much that I don't understand; if I could understand it, there wouldn't be much in it! I don't understand predestination but I believe that I am chosen in Him. I don't understand all about the security of the saints but I believe that I am a child of God and that, while my Father may discipline me, he will never disown me. I am not an expert in prophecy but I am not looking for the kingdom without the King....Too much of our orthodoxy is correct and sound but, like words without a tune, statutes without songs, it does not glow and burn, it does not stir the wells of the heart, it has lost its hallelujah, it is too much like a catechism and not enough like a camp meeting....One {woman} with a glowing experience of God is worth a library full of arguments." [6]

2. Her faith is available to anyone who truly seeks after God.

"Ask, and it shall be given you; seek, and ye shall find; and to him that knocketh it shall be opened. For every one that asketh receiveth; and he that seeketh findeth; and to him that knocketh it shall be opened." Matthew 7:7-8

3. Ellen was raised in a Christian home and believed in God her entire life, but it is never too late to believe.

"Seek ye the Lord while He may be found; call ye upon Him while He is near: Let the wicked forsake his way and the unrighteous man his thoughts: and let him return unto the Lord, and He will have mercy on him, and to our God, for He will abundantly pardon." Isaiah 55: 6-7

4. If you've come to the end of yourself and feel helpless and powerless in the face of life's challenges and hardships, turn to Jesus for help.

"'For I know the thoughts that I think for you,' saith the Lord, 'thoughts of peace, and not of evil to give you an expected end.'" Jeremiah 29:11

5. If your prayers seem to go unanswered, know that God hears all of our prayers and answers them in His own time, according to His will. Imagine Him keeping our prayers "in golden vials, like sweet incense, in His holy place in Heaven."

"Therefore I say unto you, Whatsoever things ye desire, when you pray believe that ye receive them and ye shall have them. And, when ye stand praying, forgive, if ye have ought against any; that that your Father also which is in heaven may forgive you your trespasses."
Mark 11:24-25

6. If you want to be a good person, come to Jesus, who died to make us good.
"Be ye followers of me, even as I also am of Christ."
I Corinthians 11:1

7. If you sense that there is more to life than what you can see, hear and feel, you are feeling the power and majesty of God, who created the world and cares for His creatures - the same God who planted a spark of divinity within each of us, so that, in the words of St. Augustine, "we are restless until we rest in Him."
"So God created man in His own image, in the image of God created He him; male and female created He them." Genesis 1:27

8. If you want your heart to be soft and gentle instead of hard and calloused, choose acceptance instead of resignation.
"Therefore be ye not unwise, but understanding what the will of the Lord is." Ephesians 5:17

9. Live with a thankful heart. Count your blessings. Even when times are hard, try to look on the positive side of things.

"In everything give thanks: for this is the will of God in Christ Jesus."
I Thessalonians 5:18

10. If you want to experience peace at the end of your life, then make choices for eternity at the forks in the paths of your life. Cling to Jesus and He will never forsake you. He will guide you through life's pathways and the final passageway of death.
"And the peace of God, which passeth all understanding, shall keep your hearts and minds through Christ Jesus." Philippians 4:7

Use Ellen's life as an example and remember that her Jesus is in heaven interceding for you.

APPENDIX - A Challenge

I have used many Scripture verses in this memoir. The idea of inserting the verses came to me as I wrote and became aware of the importance of the bible and prayer in my parents' lives.

I can think of no better way to honor them, than by proposing a challenge to you, my readers, young and old, to make the verses, which exemplify their lives, a part of your lives too.

The value of memorization, in improving mental acuity and warding off Alzheimer's and dementia, has been documented by medical research. Robert J. Morgan, in his book, "100 Bible Verses Everyone Should Know By Heart," describes the value of memorizing Scripture, noting that our thoughts are the most important thing about us, for we are what we think and our lives run in the direction of our thoughts. They are like seeds that produce crops. [1]

"For as he thinketh in his heart, so is he..." (Proverbs 23:7)

Morgan goes on to suggest that memorizing Scripture, and having a bank of verses at our disposal, is a means of internalizing and mainstreaming God's thoughts into our conscious, subconscious and unconscious logic. Instead of dwelling on ourselves and recycling our own thoughts, we begin to think more as God thinks, to see life from God's point of view.

"Meditation is the skeleton key that unlocks the greatest storeroom in the house of God's provision for the Christian...It is holding the Word of God in your heart until it has affected every phase of your life. Beware of getting alone with your own thoughts. Get alone with God's thoughts. There is danger in rummaging through waste and barren desert-thoughts that can be labeled—daydreaming or worse. Don't meditate upon yourself but dwell upon God...Make this a built-in habit of daily living." (From a Navigator's booklet) [2]

Starting with verses that illustrate Henry and Ellen's story should make memorization easier, since they are placed within the context of their lives. For example, the following verse was used to describe the role of Scripture in Henry's everyday life:

"This book of the law shall not depart out of thy mouth; but thou shalt meditate therein day and night, that thou mayest observe to do according to all that is written therein: for then thou shalt make thy way prosperous, and then thou shalt have good success." (Joshua 1:8)

If you will now read Psalm 1 (one of Ellen's favorite psalms), you will notice how David took this verse from Joshua, internalized it and personalized it using the image of trees planted by the rivers of water. From this verse, he then wrote Psalm 1, his meditation about meditating on Joshua 1:8. [3]

Take it one step further and visualize Henry plowing the fields by the old maple tree, mentally reciting and internalizing the Scripture verses he had memorized as he walked along, and you have a firm context for memorizing Joshua 1:8.

You will find your own system of memorization. But if you start with the verses quoted in the story, recite them and internalize them, not only will you feel closeness with Henry and Ellen, but more importantly, you will feel a closeness with the God they loved and served.

This book was meant to be a tribute to Henry and Ellen and their faith. Memorizing and internalizing the scriptures would be the highest compliment and most significant tribute we, the readers, could give them.

Ellen VanGunst, Winnie Postema and Millie Postema

Andrew and Jane VanGunst

Henry VanGunst and Ellen Postema - 1933

Henry and Ellen at Ludington State Park

Henry and Ellen VanGunst

Henry and Ellen - 50th Wedding Anniversary

Henry with Randall

A family get together at Silver Lake - 1946

Ellen Postema at home

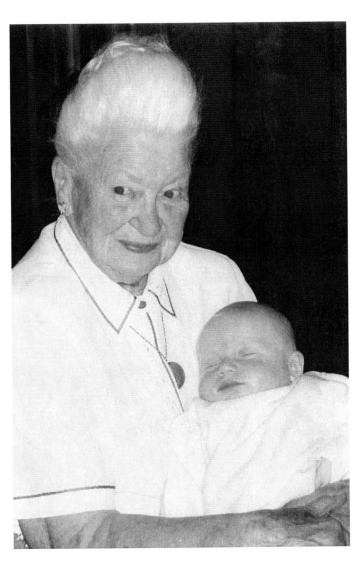

Ellen with great grandson Sam Timmer

Henry with Marilyn, Roger, Judi, Wendell and Joan

Benjamin and Winnie Postema with granddaughter, Marilyn

Henry with Randall on Maude

Henry planting the garden with Roger and Wendell

Henry and Ellen with Roger

Andrew VanGunst with Millie

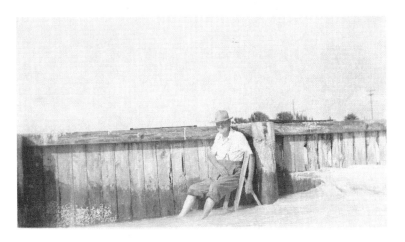

Benjamin Postema

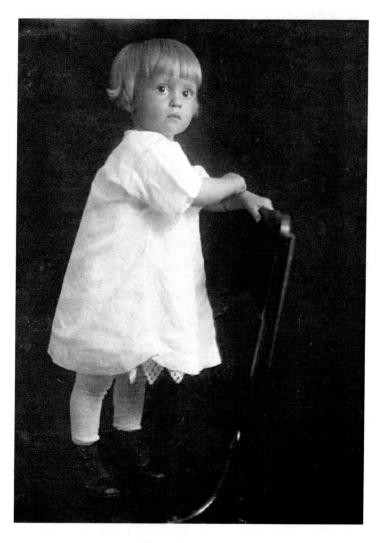

Ellen Postema

Henry in Clearwater, FL visiting Benjamin and Winnie - 1955

Ellen with Randy and Laddie - 1955

At Niagara Falls with Ellen's parents - 1952

Roger and Wendell with their milk pails

Judi, Joan, Janet and Randy with Judi's new "Blue Flyer"

Janet and Joan shoveling snow - March 1959

Jane VanGunst with Millie

Ellen VanGunst with her daughter, Janet Hasselbring

Family Tree Chart for Ellen Postema

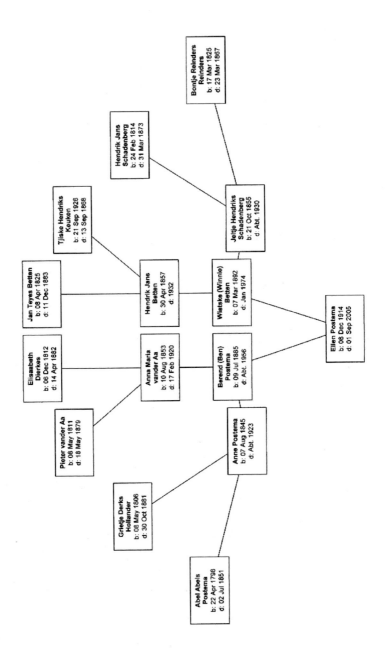

Family Tree Chart for Henry Van Gunst

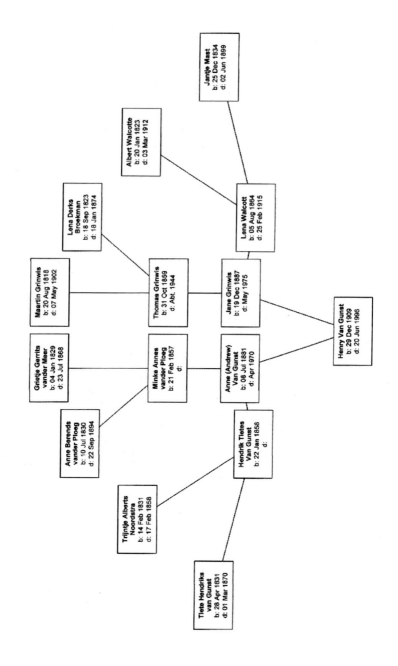

NOTES

Note: All bible references are from the King James version of the bible, the version used by Henry and Ellen.

Preface - Lighting the Match
1. Larry Woiwode, *What I Think I Did*, Basic Books, 248
2. Ibid, 266

Chapter 1 - God Will Provide
1. Henry VanDyke, *The Story of the Psalms*, 226
2. Larry Woiwode, *What I Think I Did*, Basic Books, 91
3. Vance Havner, *The Best of Vance Havner* (Baker Book House) 40, 41
4. Robert J. Morgan, *100 Bible Verses,* B & H Publishing Group, 11
5. "In the Garden," C. Austin Miles, Copyright, 1940, Rodeheaver Co., Owner
6. The Billy Graham Team, *Crusader Hymns and Hymn Stories* (The Billy Graham Evangelistic Assoc.) A Hymn Story by Don Hustad - 49, 50
7. "In the Garden," C. Austin Miles, Copyright, 1940, Rodeheaver Co., Owner
8. "In the Garden," C. Austin Miles, Copyright, 1940, Rodeheaver Co., Owner
9. T. DeWitt Talmage, *To My Mother With Thanks*, edited by Kaufman and Rosen

Chapter 4 - Heaven Tugging, Always Tugging
1. Vance Havner, "The Best of Vance Havner," Baker Book House, 41

Chapter 5 - Home at Last
1. J.R. Miller, *Unto the Hills* (Billy Graham), pg 103
2. Author unknown
3. Donna Devall, *The Power of Positive Aging*, Xlibris

    Corp., 114
4. Erwin W. Lutzer, *One Minute After You Die,* Moody Publishers, 22
5. Dwight L. Moody, "A Thoroughly Unconventional Man – The Inspirational and Entertaining Words of Dwight L. Moody," Daniel J. Favero
6. Jhabvala, "Heat and Dust"
7. William Featherston, "My Jesus I Love Thee," hymn tune

Chapter 6 - Final Gifts
1. Alexander MacLaren, *Unto the Hills* (Billy Graham), 383
2. Margery Mansfield, "Daughters Who Lose Their Mothers"
3. C.S. Lewis, "My Mother's Death."
4. Sebastian Barry, *The Secret Scripture*, pg. 297
5. C.S. Lewis, *Mere Christianity*
6. C.S. Lewis, *The Problem of Pain*
7. Charles Spurgeon, *Unto the Hills* (Billy Graham), pg. 179
8. C.S. Lewis, *Christian Behavior*
9. Laura Hillenbrand, *Unbroken*, pg. 175
10. Eckhart Tolle, *A New Earth,* pg. 9
11. Ibid, pg. 18
12. C.S. Lewis, *The Problem of Pain*
13. Laura Hillenbrand, *Unbroken*, pg. 374, 375
14. Thorton Wilder, *Unto the Hills* (Billy Graham), pg. 399
15. Vance Havner, Decision Magazine, August 2011, pg. 9
16. C.S. Lewis, From a Letter to Mrs. L
17. Vance Havner, *The Best of Vance Havner,* Baker Book House, 53
18. Dietrich Bonhoeffer, *The Cost of Discipleship,* Preface
19. Corrie TenBoom, *Unto the Hills,* pg. 90
20. Billy Graham, *Unto the Hills,* pg. 189
21. Erwin W. Lutzer, *One Minute After You Die,* pgs. 42, 43

22. Eckhart Tolle, *Practicing the Power of Now,* pg. 21
23. Dwight L. Moody, "A Thoroughly Unconventional Man – The Inspirational and Entertaining Words of Dwight L. Moody," Daniel J. Favero
24. C.S. Lewis, *The Weight of Glory*

Memories of Loved Ones
1. C.S. Lewis, *Christian Reflections,*
2. Elaine Pagels, *The Gnostic Gospels*, pg. xx, Random House, NY

Appendix

A Challenge
1. Robert J. Morgan, *100 Bible Verses,* pg. 4
2. Ibid. pg. 69
3. Ibid. Pg. 69

An Invitation
1. Robert J. Morgan, *100 Bible Verses Everyone Should Know By Heart*, pg. 56
2. Ibid. pg. 56
3. Ibid. pg. 57
4. Ibid. pg. 60
5. Ibid. pg. 64
6. Vance Havner, *The Best of Vance Havner, pp. 63, 65* Baker Book House

Study Guide I
Our Town Revisited
A Comparison of In the Garden to Thornton Wilder's Play

I. Play summary - Note: Following is a summary of *Our Town*; however, readers are urged to read the play themselves before continuing with the study.

In his classic three-act play, Wilder depicts life in the small town of Grover's Corners. Wilder's underlying theme of the transience of life and the power of time plays out through the members of the Webb and Gibbs families. Wilder juxtaposes the flurry of his characters' everyday activities with their inattentiveness to the details of their lives, demonstrating the faulty assumption, most humans have, that they have an indeterminate amount of time on Earth. Time is swiftly passing by, while the characters spend valuable amounts of it, flying back in their own minds, to past moments rather than recognizing and enjoying the value of moments, as they occur in the present, especially the details of life. The story spans many years, from 1899 to 1913; however, Wilder collapses the events into one day and depicts the whole spectrum of life - birth, companionship/marriage, and death - within the three acts of the play. Each act also encompasses a day's time, further emphasizing a human life from birth (morning) to death (evening), with the details/defining moments of one's life in between (noon). Wilder questions whether humans truly appreciate the precious nature of a transient life and the artfulness and value of everyday routine activities, such as eating breakfast, plowing a field, washing and drying dishes, milking cows, or baking bread.

The dead souls in the play chastise the living for taking these seemingly mundane actions for granted. Not even George Webb, who is grieving the absence of his wife, Emily Gibbs, who died in childbirth some years earlier, is spared their rebuke. Instead of wasting time with pitiable prostration on Em's grave, he should be enjoying what time he has left on Earth.

While Wilder emphasizes life's transience, he also shows the stability of human traditions and the steadfastness of the natural environment. He reinforces this theme by use of the hymn, "Blest Be the Tie That Binds." Sung three times, once in each act, the hymn shows another important theme of the play: the "tie that binds," refers not only to the love between God and created beings, but also to the love between humans - whether in marriage or companionship between friends, an essential, even sacred, element of human existence according to Wilder.

Probably the most dramatic event of the play occurs one morning, when Emily returns to Earth for a visit. Through the eyes of her dead soul, Wilder presents a perspective that gives this moment a truly beautiful transience and the play its best-known passage.

In *Our Town,* Wilder leaves us with a strong feeling that though mundane routines and events of our everyday lives may be repetitive, the details are what makes life interesting and deserving of our attention. His intent is to make ordinary lives seem extraordinary.

II. Comparison of *In the Garden* with *Our Town*.

Author's note: Though I had read the play, *Our Town*, in high school, I made no connection with the story when I wrote my mother's memoir, *In the Garden*. It was only when I was working on the "Questions for Discussion/Meditation" sections of the memoir, and specifically, the section "A New Heaven" (Final Gifts, Section 5), that I remembered the play's famous quote, spoken by Em, when she returned to Earth for a visit on her twelfth birthday. "Do human beings ever realize life while they live it- every, every minute?" she asks rhetorically, of the audience. Then, the play and it's themes of the transience of life, the swift passing of time, the importance of human "ties," and Wilder's overall intention of making ordinary lives extraordinary, by paying attention to the details, came back to me. I realized, with some amazement, that these were the same themes I had used in the memoir. The similarities are many - both stories are set in small towns (Grover's Corners and New Era), both feature the lives of two families, (the Webbs and the Gibbs; the Postemas and the Van Gunsts), both take place in the early 1900s, both describe the spectrum of human lives (Ellen's life is described from birth, to marriage, to parenthood, to death), and lastly - uncannily, in both, childbirth plays a dominant role (Em died in childbirth, while Ellen was advised that she would die if she carried her seventh baby, Randall, to term).

III. Questions for Discussion/Meditation/Journaling.

With this background, consider the following quotations from *Our Town* and their relevance to *In the Garden* and specifically to Ellen and Henry's lives.
1. "So--people a thousand years from now - this is the way we were in the provinces north of New York at the beginning of the twentieth century. - This is the way we were: in our growing up and in our marrying and in our living and in our dying." (Stage Manager, Act 1) While many plays deal with dramatic, heightened emotion or important historical events, Wilder addresses daily events and traditional, recognizable ceremonies. In his address to future readers, he reveals his hope that the play will provide a lasting testimony to the importance of appreciating the simple details in life.
Study question: Did Ellen and Henry appreciate the simple details of life? What might people "a thousand years from now," gain from reading about their lives?
2. "People are meant to go through life two by two. Tain't natural to be lonesome."
(Mrs.Gibbs, Act II) Here Wilder articulates one of the play's central themes: the sanctity of human interactions, both in marriage and other relationships, such as companionship, care, and compassion. He seems to place the nonromantic friendships above the romantic.
Study question: What were the romantic and nonromantic relationships in Ellen and Henry's lives. Discuss the place these relationships had on their lives.
3. "I think that once you've found a person that you're very fond of...I mean a person who's fond of you, too, and likes you enough to be interested in your character...Well I think that's just as important as college is, and even more

so. That's what I think." (George, speaking to Emily, Act II) Wilder's play is as much about community as it is about individual achievement and experience. Here he suggests that higher education may not be a natural stage in human development as love is.

Study question: How does this theme play out in Ellen's and Henry's lives, neither of whom went to school beyond high school?

4. "We all know that something is eternal. And it ain't houses and it ain't names, and it ain't earth, and it ain't even the stars...everybody knows in their bones that something is eternal, and that something has to do with human beings. All the greatest people ever lived have been telling us that for five thousand years and yet you'd be surprised how people are always losing hold of it. There's something way down deep that's eternal about every human being...Aren't they waitin' for the eternal part in them to come out clear?" (Stage Manager, Act III) Humans possess eternity in their souls and can share this eternal nature through their daily interactions with one another, but they get caught up in the day-to-day details, missing the meaningful nature of human existence. Wilder suggests that human interaction may exceed even the unfathomable beauty of the afterlife.

Study question: Did Ellen and Henry understand the true significance of existence and recognize the eternal in the daily chores and routines of their daily lives? Find specific examples in the memoir to support your answer.

5. "Do human beings ever realize life while they live it - every, every minute?" (Emily, Act III) As Emily returns to Earth on her twelfth birthday, she tries - although futilely, to get her mother to look at her and not take her presence for granted. Feeling pained by the recognition that human

beings waste great opportunities at every moment, Emily returns to the cemetery. With the play's best-known passage, Wilder concludes his argument that people lack a sense of wonder at eternity passing before their eyes every day.

Study question: Did Ellen and Henry "realize life while they lived it?" Give specific examples from the memoir to support your position (with help from SparkNotes).

Study Guide II
Chapter by Chapter

Chapter 1 - God Will Provide

Questions for Discussion/Meditation/Journaling

1. "So Boaz said to Ruth, "...Don't go and glean in another field and don't go away from here. Stay here with the women who work for me. Watch the field where the men are harvesting, and follow along after the women. I have told the men not to lay a hand on you. And whenever you are thirsty, go and get a drink from the water jars the men have filled." Ruth 2: 8 - 9 (NIV) Knowing what you do about Andrew's hardships, being orphaned as a child, working for room and board and finally earning enough money to buy land of his own, can you understand his somewhat parsimonious attitude toward his only son, Henry, and his and Jane's apparent dislike/distrust of Ellen? Do you suppose Ellen was partly responsible for the situation?

2. "...since what may be known about God is plain to them, because God has made it plain to them. For since the creation of the world God's invisible qualities—his eternal power and divine nature—have been clearly seen, being understood from what has been made, so that people are without excuse." Romans 1:19 - 20 (NIV) Ellen grew up in a religious home and attended church, Sunday School, and catechism (religious instruction), but when she married and moved to the farm with Henry, her religious experience became intensely personal and spiritual. To what do you attribute this change?

3. "For the love of money is a root of all kinds of evil. Some people, eager for money, have wandered from the faith and pierced themselves with many griefs. I Timothy 6: 9 - 11 (NIV) "Come, all you who are thirsty, come to the waters; and you who have no money, come, buy and eat! Come, buy wine and milk without money and without cost." Isaiah 55:1-3 (NIV) Henry and Ellen eked out a living on the farm and were poor by earthly standards, with lack of money continually an issue; yet, their faith seemed to become deeper and stronger. Was this because of, or despite, their dire financial straits? Discuss the role poverty played in the development of their faith. Based on their story, can poverty ever be viewed as positive? Conversely, is wealth a negative? Do you think it is easier to follow Jesus being rich or poor?

4. "Remember those earlier days after you had received the light, when you endured in a great conflict full of suffering." Hebrews 10:32 (NIV) Reread the scenario on page 58, where Ellen and Henry are struggling with the issue of Ellen's pregnancy with Randall and the doctor's advice that if she carries the baby to term, she may die. Presented, as they were, with two unacceptable options - ending a sacred life, or Henry losing his precious Ellen and being left to raise seven children on his own, imagine them discussing the pros and cons of this complicated situation.

5. "...And, who knows but that you have come to {be born} for such a time as this?" Esther 4:14 (NIV) Ellen's story is not unique. There are many - especially women, who have endured loss, suffering, and hardship. Do you think Ellen's story is unique? Discuss Ellen's personality and character and what about her makes her life "extraordinary."

6. Madeleine L'Engle notes that one can react to

suffering and pain with either acceptance or resignation, but she cautions that the choice will make all the difference in one's life. Think about how that choice played out in Ellen's life and contributed to the person she became. Then discuss the difference between the choices - acceptance and resignation, the fine line that separates them, and why the choice for acceptance is so crucial to one's faith. Think of a time when you were at a fork in the road of your life and how you responded. Did you choose acceptance or resignation? If you didn't choose acceptance, and would like another chance, know that you can always begin anew. Are acceptance and redemption alike in some way?

7. Discuss Ellen's walking and talking "in the garden" with her Lord. Why did the author add these passages to the story? What role do they play in painting a picture of Ellen's life and faith? Do you have "in the garden," experiences when you walk and talk with your Lord? If so, is there a special place where you feel close to God? If not, do you think you would want to establish such a place for meeting and talking with God? Where might that place be for you?

Chapter 2 - Accepting the Unacceptable

Questions for Discussion/Meditation/Journaling

1. Read Luke 22. How is Ellen's experience of dealing with her daughter Judi's death like Jesus' experience in the garden, before His crucifixion and death, when he prayed to His heavenly Father: "He was withdrawn from them about a stone's cast, and kneeled down and prayed, saying, Father, if thou be willing, remove this cup from me: nevertheless not my will, but Thine, be done." Luke 22: 41 - 42 (NIV)

2. Read Mark 15 and also the story of Jonah. "And he bought fine linen, and took him down, and wrapped him in the linen and laid him in a sepulchre which was hewn out of a rock, and rolled a stone unto the door of the sepulchre." Mark 15:46 (NIV) "For as Jonah was three days and three nights in the whale's belly; so shall the Son of Man will be three days and three nights in the heart of the earth." Matthew 12:40 (NIV) What is the significance of Ellen's withdrawal to her room after hearing of the death of Judi?

3. Read the resurrection story in Matthew 28. Do you see any connection between Ellen's emergence from her room after days of seclusion and the story of the resurrection? "The angel answered and said unto to the women, Fear not ye: For I know that ye seek Jesus, which was crucified. He is not here: for he is risen, as he said..." Matthew 28: 5 -6 (NIV)

4. "Jesus said unto her, I am the resurrection and the life: he that believeth in me, though he were dead, yet shall he live: And whosoever liveth and believeth in me shall never die. Believest thou this?" John 11: 25 - 26 (NIV) Describe the resurrection that occurred in Ellen's life. How did this come about?

5. "And we know that all things work together for good to them that love God, to them who are the called according to his purpose." Romans 8:28 (NIV) How does this verse exemplify Ellen's life after the death of Judi?

6 "For I know the plans I have for you," declares the Lord, "plans to prosper you and not to harm you, plans to give you a future and a hope." Jeremiah 29:11 (NIV) Using this verse, think of experiences in your life, with family or friends that are similar to Ellen's experience in the loss of her daughter, Judi. Can you find ways that God

was/is present to you in times of tragedy and loss?

7. From what you know of how placement in the family affects a child's development, do you think being the third child could have had anything to do with Judi's problems?

8. So little was known about mental illness, specifically depression, back when Judi was having problems. How have methods for treating mental illness changed since then? Do you think society's attitude toward mental illness has changed?

Chapter 3 - Living With Estrangement

Questions for Discussion/Meditation/Journaling

1. From the narrative, you know that Randall did return home from Viet Nam after his time was up, and he seemed to be settling in on the farm. What do you think could have motivated him to reenlist?

2. With what you know about war and its effects on soldiers and from the facts given in the narrative, what do you think caused Randall's sudden refusal to speak to his mother, Ellen, (after he had reenlisted) and then to become estranged from her and his family?

3. Reread the accounts of Wendell and Roger visiting Randall and being treated as total strangers. How can war cause a soldier to lose all emotional connection with those close to him, so that his/her sense of bonding is erased?

4. Compare the Viet Nam war with other wars our country has fought. How were the circumstances of that war, and the attitude of the country towards the war, different than what existed at the time of the Viet Nam conflict? How could those differences have contributed to Randall's situation - settling in Washington and becoming estranged from his family?

4. Have you known a friend or family member who went to war? How was their experience like Randall's? How was it different?

5. The author mentions that it might have been easier for Ellen if Randall had died in the jungles of Viet Nam. Do you agree? Why or why not?

6. Reread pages 83 and 84 and the words from I John 4:19: "We love him, because he first loved us." Ellen's response to Randall's estrangement causes us to reflect on the types of love - platonic love - the love of friends and fellowship; romantic love - covering everything from queasy stomachs and warm fuzzy feelings to strong sensual passion; and agape love - which, unlike the other two, is not limited or held hostage by someone's perception or the environment, but rather involves a decision to proactively seek someone else's well-being. Agape is a spiritual, compassionate, ego-less, self-giving love, offered without concern for personal gain or reward. The lover loves without expectation of personal gain or reward, obviously, difficult to achieve by mere mortals. Discuss whether Ellen's love for Randall reached the level of unqualified love - agape love, practiced and preached by Jesus, Buddha, and Gandhi. Do you agree with some, that maternal love is, by definition, agape love? Why/why not?

Chapter 4 - Heaven Tugging, Always Tugging

Questions for Discussion/Meditation/Journaling

1. "Now we have received, not the spirit of the world, but the spirit which is of God, which is in him. Even so the things of God knoweth no man, but the spirit of God." I Corinthians 2:12 (NIV) The author noted that tragedy can force many couples to grow apart and separate; however,

the tragedy of Judi's death and Randall's estrangement only brought Henry and Ellen closer together. What accounts for couples to separate in difficult times? What was the difference for Henry and Ellen?

2. "The Lord is my Shepherd, I shall not want. He maketh me to lie down in green pastures: he leadeth me beside the still waters. He restoreth my soul: he leadeth me in the paths of righteousness for his namesake." Psalm 23:1-3 (NIV) What part did Henry's closeness with nature play in his relationship with his Lord in life and in death?

3. "Let your conversation be without covetousness; and be content with such things as ye have." Hebrews 13:5 (NIV) Poverty and hardship can turn some people into parsimonious, stingy, and miserly people. What was the difference with Henry and Ellen, who were always struggling to make ends meet, yet, were generous, kind hearted, and content with what they had?

4. The author alludes to the fact that Ellen, a newcomer to the farm, was often the one comforting Henry (who had lived on the farm his entire life), in the face of hardship. How do you account for Ellen being the emotionally stronger of the two?

5. "And Elimelech, Naomi's husband died and she was left...I went out full, and the Lord hath brought me home again empty: why then call ye me, Naomi, seeing the Lord hath testified against me, and the Almighty hath afflicted me?" Ruth 1:3; 1:21 (NIV) What was the secret of Henry and Ellen's love affair of 60+ years?

Chapter 5 - Home At Last

Questions for Discussion/Meditation/Journaling

1. Reread pages 115 and 116. Here the author ventures

an explanation for the quote, "But we are in mourning for our mothers before even we are born," by Sebastian Barry in his book, *The Secret Scripture.* Do you agree with her explanation? Discuss the implications of this quote generally and in the light of your relationship with your mother.

2. Consider these verses: "The grass withered, the flower fadeth..." Isaiah 40:7 (NIV) and "For I know the plans I have for you," declares the Lord, "plans to prosper you and not to harm you, plans to give you a future and a hope." Jeremiah 29:11 (NIV) At the end of her life, Ellen had come full circle, experiencing the dependency and helplessness of a baby in the womb. Discuss how God's plans for Ellen played out from beginning to end - from birth to death. How has this verse, from Jeremiah, been significant in your life, in the life of your mother, or in the life of someone you love or are close to?

3. Using the same verse from Jeremiah 29:11, review the defining moments of Ellen's life - birth, marriage to Henry, life on the farm, loss of Judi and estrangement from Randall, Henry's death, her own failing health and finally, her death. Having read the narrative, would you add any other defining moments to this list? Reflect on how she reacted to each of life's experiences, paying attention to Madeleine L'Engle's differentiation between acceptance and resignation and the difference the choice makes in one's life. Then, make a list of the defining moments in your own life and reflect on how you dealt with each, acceptance or resignation, and the resulting implications for your life. Do the same with the life of your mother and/or the lives of others you know.

4. "Nevertheless I am continually with thee: thou hast holden me by my right hand. Thou shalt guide me with thy

counsel, and afterward receive me to glory. Whom have I in heaven but thee? and there is none upon earth that I desire beside thee." Psalm 73:23-25 (NIV) In the light of God's glory and grace in dealing with His children, reread the author's description of C.S. Lewis's allegory, *The Great Divorce,* on pg. vii of the preface. Review Ellen's life and reflect on what caused her to be like the one soul on the bus who remained in the heavenly heights, while the rest of the pilgrims chose to return to their home in the gray "Shadowlands," the world of mediocrity, compromise and probably resignation. Read *The Great Divorce* and reflect on your life and the choices you've made at the forks in your pilgrimage, then imagine yourself on the busload of pilgrims. Would you remain in the heavenly heights with the one brave soul or return with the majority to the Shadowlands?

Chapter 6 - Final Gifts

Questions for Discussion/Meditation/Journaling

1. A Life of Faith - Reflect on Spurgeon's quote on page 114: "We can learn nothing of the gospel, except by feeling its truths." What does this mean? From what you have learned about Ellen and Henry's lives, how does this quote play out in Ellen's life? In Henry's life? In your life or the life of someone you know?

2. Suffering -
   a. Compare the psalmist's cries of despair in the following verses: "My God, my God, why hast Thou forsaken me?" from Psalm 22 and "Have mercy on me, O God; have mercy on me, for in You my soul takes refuge. I will take refuge in the shadow of Your wings until the

disaster has passed," from Psalm 57, when David was hiding from Saul in the cave. Note the utter desperation of the first with the more somber, almost serene, prayer of the second, which has an underlying element of trust. It has been suggested that the first prayer is calamitous, while the second is more of a peaceful, though certainly somber, nature. Reflect on Ellen's prayers with her God, "in the garden." Which would you characterize as calamitous, like Psalm 22, and which more peaceful in nature, as in Psalm 54? Have you known times of despair when you cried out to God for help? Were your cries calamitous or serene in nature?

b. Reread C.S. Lewis's quote on page 118: "God whispers to us in our pleasures, speaks in our conscience, but shouts in our pains; it is His megaphone to rouse a deaf world." Reflect on times in your life when God whispered, spoke, and/or shouted to you. Do you agree with Lewis's observation?

3. Indwelling of the Holy Spirit - Reread pages. 40-42. Vance Havner, the country preacher, reexamines the word, "culture," suggesting that, for too long, it has meant, "college degrees, ability to talk about art and literature, several trips abroad and proficiency in etiquette." (Pleasant Paths, pg. 84) He suggests a new standard, based on Solomon's wisdom in Proverbs 16:32: "{She} that ruleth {her} spirit is better than he that taketh a city," and John's admonition that God would have us prosper only as our souls prosper (III John 2). Ellen didn't go to college and even though she had access to the "cultural" niceties of art, literature, travel, and etiquette while growing up, she left that world behind when she married Henry, moved to the farm, and struggled just to make ends meet. It was there,

she yielded her life to Jesus and invited Him into her heart. Then, filled with the Spirit, she bore the fruits of love, joy, peace, long-suffering, gentleness, goodness, faith, meekness and temperance - true marks of culture. Reflect on each attribute of the Spirit above and how it was demonstrated in Ellen's life.

4. Discipleship -

a. "...And, who knows but that you have come to{be born}for such a time as this?" Esther 4:14 (NIV) Ellen's story is not unique. There are many - especially women, who have endured loss, suffering and hardship. Do you agree that Ellen's life was extraordinary? Discuss her personality and character, and what about her makes her life "extraordinary."

b. Again, consider Mordacai's words to Esther as you reflect on the lives of great people in history, and what made them extraordinary. How were they "born for such a time as this?"

5. A New Heaven - Some view a belief in heaven as a crutch for the weak of faith and faint of heart. Is heaven, indeed, a place, or do you agree with Tolle's description, that heaven is an inner realm of consciousness? Is there a sense that heaven and hell can begin right now, based on how one lives.? Think of someone near to you who has died. Do you envision them dwelling in a place?

6. A Serene Holy Life -

a. Consider Tolle's description of ego as a false self (*In the Garden*, page 136) and the truth that "nothing real will ever be lost." Think of experiences when you were moved beyond yourself to the realm of the sacred, where you realized the truth that "nothing real will ever be lost." What made those experiences special and sacred?

    b. Reflect on Ellen's life - an ordinary woman becoming extraordinary because of her complete trust in her Lord. What does her story mean to you? Does it change you or inspire you in some way. Compare her life with that of your mother, grandmother, someone close to you or even yourself. Write your own memoir of this person's life.

Chapter – A Final Word

1. "If our heart condemns us, God is greater than our heart, and knows all things." I John 3:20 (NIV) The author's letter to her mother is obviously a story of forgiveness, reconciliation, resurrection, and redemption. Discuss the human and divine aspects of each as they played out in the author's life, specifically in her relationship with her mother.

2. "But we are in mourning for our mothers, even before we are born." (Sebastian Barry, *The Secret Scripture*). If you were to write a letter to your mother, what would it say? If she is living, you have the privilege of giving it to her. If she is no longer living, it can serve as a powerful means of reflecting on your relationship with her.

Author's note:

It is my hope and prayer that you have been blessed by this story of my mother's extraordinary life and that the study guides have enhanced your appreciation and understanding of her story.

I am available to review/discuss the memoir with bible study groups, the Coffee Break Program, book clubs and other presentations, offering a message of inspiration and hope.

You may contact me at janhasselbring@yahoo.com or at 616-402-0961.

Notes:

Notes:

Notes:

Notes: